Amílcar Cabral

OHIO SHORT HISTORIES OF AFRICA

This series of Ohio Short Histories of Africa is meant for those who are looking for a brief but lively introduction to a wide range of topics in African history, politics, and biography, written by some of the leading experts in their fields.

Amílcar Cabral

*A Nationalist and
Pan-Africanist Revolutionary*

Peter Karibe Mendy

OHIO UNIVERSITY PRESS

ATHENS

Ohio University Press, Athens, Ohio 45701
ohioswallow.com
© 2019 by Ohio University Press
All rights reserved

Printed in the United States of America
Ohio University Press books are printed on acid-free paper ⊗ ™

29 28 27 26 25 24 23 22 21 20 19   5 4 3 2 1

Cover design by Joey Hifi

Library of Congress Cataloging-in-Publication Data
Names: Mendy, Peter Michael Karibe, author.
Title: Amílcar Cabral : a nationalist and pan-Africanist revolutionary /
  Peter Karibe Mendy.
Other titles: Ohio short histories of Africa.
Description: Athens : Ohio University Press, 2019. | Series: Ohio short
  histories of Africa | Includes bibliographical references and index.
Identifiers: LCCN 2019004321| ISBN 9780821423721 (pb : alk. paper)
| ISBN
  9780821446621 (pdf)
Subjects: LCSH: Cabral, Amílcar, 1924-1973. |
  Guinea-Bissau--History--Revolution, 1963-1974. | Cabo Verde--His-
tory--To 1975. | Partido Africano da Independência da Guiné e Cabo
Verde. | National liberation movements--Guinea-Bissau--History--20th
century. | National liberation movements--Cabo Verde--History--20th
century. | Revolutionaries--Guinea-Bissau--Biography.
Classification: LCC DT613.76.C3 M46 2019 | DDC 966.5702092--dc23
LC record available at https://lccn.loc.gov/2019004321

Contents

Illustrations

Maps

Figures

Preface and Acknowledgments

The assassination of Amílcar Cabral, the charismatic leader of the African Party for the Independence of Guinea and Cabo Verde (PAIGC), on 20 January 1973, and the unilateral declaration of the independence of Guinea-Bissau by his liberation movement eight months later, were critical turning points that greatly sharpened my political consciousness. I was born in Gambia, West Africa, during the terminal period of British colonial rule. Both my parents were natives of Guinea-Bissau, then called Portuguese Guinea, located about four hundred miles south. Like thousands of others before them, they left their homeland to escape the harsher colonial order there characterized by forced labor and corporal punishment. While the Portuguese were not the only European colonizers in Africa to maintain the *pax colonica* by brutal repression, they were nevertheless the last to formally end it, in 1961, following the uprisings in Angola that signaled the beginning of armed national liberation struggle there.

Growing up in Gambia before the start of the war of independence in Guinea-Bissau, I heard numerous stories from newly arrived family members of colonial abuse and violence meted out to the majority of the population, contemptuously called *gentios* (heathens). As a student in England during the 1970s, I keenly followed the unfolding brutal war that became known as "Portugal's Vietnam" because of the huge Portuguese troop concentration, the dropping of napalm and white phosphorous bombs, and the removing and resettling of villagers in heavily guarded camps fenced by barbed wire. I also kept abreast of the development of the armed struggle by way of publications obtained from the Mozambique Angola Guiné Information Centre (MAGIC) in London and presentations by Basil Davidson at the Centre of West African Studies at the University of Birmingham, England, where I was a politically active graduate student.

The remarkable achievements of Cabral, who was an accomplished agronomist, an ardent nationalist, an astute diplomat, a brilliant military strategist, a committed Pan-Africanist, and an outspoken internationalist, became an enduring source of inspiration for me. As a revolutionary leader, Cabral remains as significant as his celebrated contemporaries, notably Mao Zedong, Frantz Fanon, Fidel Castro, and Ernesto "Che" Guevara.

A lot has been written about Cabral. Many of the studies are excellent scholarly analyses of him as a revolutionary theoretician and practitioner and of his achievements and legacy. In the English-speaking world, the pioneering work of Basil Davidson, *The Liberation of*

Guiné: Aspects of an African Revolution (1969), inspired or provoked such studies as *Amílcar Cabral: Revolutionary Leadership and People's War* (1983) by Patrick Chabal, *Amílcar Cabral's Revolutionary Theory and Practice: A Critical Guide* (1991) by Ronald H. Chilcote, and *Warriors at Work: How Guinea Was Really Set Free* (1993) by Mustafah Dhada.

However, since most people are not scholars, the findings of scholarship have remained confined to a small group of specialists and general readers. One of Africa's most original thinkers and politically influential figures, Cabral is little known in the Anglophone world. The notable contributions of this creatively pensive and charismatic African leader have yet to be found in high school or college textbooks. In the context of a rapidly globalizing and increasingly unequal world, his insistence that national liberation should not end with "flag independence" but should also empower people to consistently improve their material wellbeing has significance far beyond Africa. The enormous challenges he faced, and the successful approaches and strategies he deployed to find solutions, provide great opportunities to learn important lessons pertinent to the daily struggles of millions of people in the world toiling under the heavy weight of poverty, exploitation, and oppression. A visionary and inspirational leader, his ideas still resonate today. Yet, his life, charismatic leadership qualities, and accomplishments are largely unknown outside the Lusophone world. This short biography is an attempt to address this deficit.

It is singularly appropriate that a book on the life of Amílcar Cabral narrated against the background of his times should be included in the Ohio Short Histories of Africa series. The biographical profile sketched out in the pages that follow will provide some insight into the intensively lived life of a remarkable self-styled "simple African" who became a leading founding father of two independent African nations.

I remain enormously grateful to the Ohio University Press series editor Gillian Berchowitz for providing me the great opportunity to write this book as a contribution. I am also greatly thankful to Gillian for her infinite patience and professional guidance and to Nancy Basmajian, managing editor, for supervising the skillful editing of the manuscript. Further thanks are due to the two anonymous reviewers of the manuscript for their insightful critical comments. This book is based on my own studies on Amílcar Cabral and the colonial and postcolonial periods in Guinea-Bissau, but I am very much indebted to the corpus of research and publications on this important historical figure. I owe a special debt of gratitude to the veterans of the armed liberation struggle in Guinea-Bissau who generously granted me interviews to share their valuable intimate knowledge and memories of Cabral; in particular, I am very grateful to Manuel "Manecas" dos Santos, Lúcio Soares, Samba Lamine Mané, Carmen Pereira (who died on June 4, 2016, six months after granting me an interview), Teodora Inácia Gomes, Douda Bangura, and

Florentino "Flora" Gomes. I am also particularly grateful to Iva Cabral for her prompt response to my request for images of her father, which she generously provided, with kind identification of the photographers and the copyright holders. I remain beholden to my family, including my extended kindred in Guinea-Bissau, for their unfailing support. Ultimately, I take full responsibility for errors of fact and interpretation as well as translation of quoted Portuguese texts.

This book is dedicated to the young generation of committed nationalist and Pan-Africanist *Cabralistas* engaged in life-threatening struggles for social and economic justice, peace, prosperity, and the rights-based unification of the diverse peoples of Africa.

Abbreviations and Acronyms

ANP   Assembleia Nacional Popular (People's National Assembly)

CEA   Centro de Estudos Africanos (Center for African Studies)

CEI   Casa dos Estudantes do Império (House of Students of the Empire)

CEL   Conselho Executívo da Luta (Executive Council of the Struggle)

CFAO   Compagnie Française de l'Afrique Occidentale (French West Africa Company)

CLSTP   Comité de Libertação de São Tomé e Príncipe (Committee for the Liberation of São Tomé and Príncipe)

CONCP   Conferência das Organizações Nacionalistas das Colónias Portuguesas (Conference of the Nationalist Organizations of the Portuguese Colonies)

CSL   Conselho Superior da Luta (Higher Council of the Struggle)

CUF   Companhia União Fabril (Union Manufacturing Company)

DGS	Direção-Geral de Segurança (Directorate-General of Security)
FAP	Força Aérea Portuguesa (Portuguese Air Force)
FARP	Forças Armadas Revolucionárias do Povo (People's Revolutionary Armed Forces)
FLING	Frente de Luta pela Independência Nacional da Guiné (Front for Struggle for the National Independence of Guinea)
FLN	Front de Libération Nationale (National Liberation Front)
FLNG	Front de Libération Nationale de la Guinée (Guinean National Liberation Front)
FNLA	Frente Nacional de Libertação de Angola (National Front for the Liberation of Angola)
FRAIN	Frente Revolucionária Africana para a Independência Nacional das Colónias Portuguesas (African Revolutionary Front for the National Independence of the Portuguese Colonies)
FRELIMO	Frente de Libertação de Moçambique (Liberation Front of Mozambique)
FUL	Front Uni de Libération [de la Guinée et du Cap Vert] (United Liberation Front [of Guinea and Cabo Verde])
ISA	Instituto Superior de Agronomia (Higher Institute of Agronomy)
MAC	Movimento Anti-Colonialista (Anticolonialist Movement)

MDCP	Movimento Democrático das Colónias Portuguesas (Democratic Movement of the Portuguese Colonies)
MFA	Movimento das Forças Armadas (Armed Forces Movement)
MING	Movimento para Independência Nacional da Guiné Portuguesa (Movement for the National Independence of Portuguese Guinea)
MLG	Movimento de Libertação da Guiné (Liberation Movement of Guinea)
MLNCP	Movimento de Libertação Nacional das Colónias Portuguesas (National Liberation Movement of the Portuguese Colonies)
MMCG	Misión Militar Cubana en Guinea y Guinea-Bissau (Cuban Military Mission in Guinea and Guinea-Bissau)
MPLA	Movimento Popular de Libertação de Angola (Popular Movement for the Liberation of Angola)
MUD	Movimento de Unidade Democrática (Movement of Democratic Unity)
MUDJ	Movimento de Unidade Democrática Juvenil (Youth Movement of Democratic Unity)
NATO	North Atlantic Treaty Organization
OAU	Organization of African Unity
PAI	Partido Africano da Independência (African Independence Party)

PAIGC	Partido Africano da Independência da Guiné e Cabo Verde (African Party for the Independence of Guinea and Cabo Verde)
PCP	Partido Comunista Português (Portuguese Communist Party)
PIDE	Polícia Internacional e de Defesa do Estado (International and State Defense Police)
PLUAA	Partido da Luta Unida dos Africanos de Angola (Party of the Unified Struggle of the Africans of Angola)
PRC	People's Republic of China
PS	Partido Socialista (Socialist Party) (Portugal)
PSP	Polícia de Segurança Pública (Public Security Police)
SIDA	Swedish International Development Agency
UDEMU	União Democrática das Mulheres (Women's Democratic Union)
UNGP	União dos Naturais da Guiné Portuguesa (Union of the Natives of Portuguese Guinea)
UPA	União das Populações de Angola (Union of the Peoples of Angola)
UPGP	União das Populações da Guiné dita Portuguesa (Union of the Populations of So-Called Portuguese Guinea)
UPLG	União Popular para Libertação da Guiné (Popular Union for the Liberation of Guinea)
USSR	Union of Soviet Socialist Republics

Introduction

Amílcar Lopes Cabral was among the iconic political leaders of the twentieth century. A consummate nationalist and Pan-Africanist revolutionary, he masterminded the end of Portuguese rule in Guinea-Bissau and Cabo Verde and was also actively engaged in the anticolonial struggles in Angola, Mozambique, and São Tomé and Príncipe. The protracted armed struggle waged by his liberation movement, the African Party for the Independence of Guinea and Cabo Verde (PAIGC), bestowed upon Guinea-Bissau a central role that defined the course and outcome of the decolonization process in the other Portuguese African colonies.

Cabral was born in Guinea-Bissau in 1924 of parents from the island of Santiago in Cabo Verde. The ten-island archipelago was reached and settled by the Portuguese in the fifteenth century. The slave plantation society that was established there was the prototype of what the Americas would later become. When slavery was abolished in 1869 it was replaced by an equally exploitative system that included the use of poor Cabo Verdean *contratados* (indentured laborers) in the cacao plantations of São Tomé and Príncipe. On the other hand, as the main beneficiary of Portugal's educational enterprise in Africa, with a seminary opened on the island of São Nicolau in 1866, Cabo Verde had the lowest illiteracy rate in Portuguese Africa: in 1959, it was 78 percent, compared to 97 percent in Angola, 98 percent in Mozambique, and 99 percent in Portuguese Guinea. The much higher literacy rate in the archipelago largely accounted for the predominance of Cabo Verdeans in the colonial administration of Portuguese Guinea, Cabral's *terra natal* (land of birth), from where, at age eight, he moved to his *terra ancestral* (ancestral land).

In 1945, following the completion of his high school education in Cabo Verde, Cabral left for Portugal and enrolled as an agronomy student at the Technical University of Lisbon, where he graduated in 1950. While in Lisbon he actively engaged in clandestine antistate politics together with other radicalized African students, including Agostinho Neto and Mário Pinto de Andrade from Angola, and Marcelino dos Santos from Mozambique.

Cabral returned to Portuguese Guinea in 1952 to work as an agronomist. For two years he traveled extensively in the colony to conduct its first agricultural census. This gave him the opportunity to learn about the colonial realities experienced by the colonized. His seminal study on land use, crop cultivation, and, among other things, soil conditions, remains a work of reference. But perhaps more important for Cabral was the acquisition of strategic knowledge about the level of discontent among his compatriots, and the likely responses to an anticolonial mobilization drive for independence.

As the leader of the PAIGC he cofounded in 1956, Cabral became a key player in the political, military, and diplomatic battles that had to be won in order to guarantee victory for the armed struggle that was launched in January 1963, following unsuccessful attempts at peaceful decolonization. His true genius was his ability to mobilize and inspire his fellow compatriots to take life-threatening risks. He was also adept at persuading skeptical international opinion of the righteousness of the armed struggle in the context of an intensifying Cold War, and thus able to secure vital political support and material resources without ties and compromises.

A committed Pan-Africanist, Cabral also played a significant role in the establishment of two of the most effective liberation movements in Angola and Mozambique, respectively the Popular Movement for the Liberation of Angola (MPLA) and the Liberation Front of Mozambique (FRELIMO). He was also a cofounder and the spokesperson of the three successive coalitions of liberation movements in Portuguese Africa, namely the Anticolonialist Movement (MAC), the African Revolutionary Front for the National Independence of the Portuguese Colonies (FRAIN), and the Conference of the Nationalist Organizations of the Portuguese Colonies (CONCP).

Cabral consistently expressed his commitment to and solidarity with "every just cause" in the world, from the Vietnam conflict to the Congo crisis, from the civil rights struggles in the United States to the Palestinian movement for statehood. At the same time, he wrote a number of brilliant works on liberation theory and practice, culture, African history, and class formation, for which he received international acclaim and many awards and honors, including honorary doctorates from Lincoln University in the United States and the Soviet Academy of Science in the then Union of Soviet Socialist Republics (USSR).

Notwithstanding his assassination, Cabral's liberation movement was able to proclaim the independence of Guinea-Bissau, on 24 September 1973, which was quickly recognized by over eighty countries around the world. The military and diplomatic victory of the PAIGC contributed significantly to the downfall of the forty-eight-year-old fascist dictatorship in Portugal called the Estado Novo (New State) and the rapid dismantlement of the Portuguese empire in Africa. When viewed against the background of a raging Cold War and the stubbornness of a well-armed NATO member nation bent on maintaining its "overseas provinces" at all costs, Cabral's achievements are indeed remarkable. His ideas, effective charismatic leadership, and achievements are memorialized in many countries in Africa and beyond.

This book aims to demonstrate the importance of leadership by focusing on the political and intellectual challenges and accomplishments of one of Africa's most effective leaders of the twentieth century. Cabral's importance lies in the fact that (i) he competently organized and led one of Africa's most consequential armed liberation struggles, (ii) he skillfully mobilized more than a dozen ethnic groups into a united binationalist cause, (iii) he ably led a successful united front against Portuguese colonialism in Africa, and (iv) he wrote incisive essays and innovative books that still resonate today.

1

Terra Natal

Early Childhood in Portuguese Guinea, 1924–32

Amílcar Lopes Cabral was born on 12 September 1924 in Bafatá, Portuguese Guinea, the mainland of which was finally conquered by Portugal only nine years earlier. The longstanding "pacification" campaigns that preceded the Berlin Conference of 1884–85 and intensified after 1912 with the arrival of the conquistador Captain João Teixeira Pinto eventually ended with the conquest of the adjacent eighty-eight-island Bijagós archipelago in 1936.

Located in West Africa and wedged between Senegal to the north and east, the Republic of Guinea (also known as Guinea-Conakry) to the south, and the Atlantic Ocean to the west, the area now known as Guinea-Bissau (36,130 square kilometers / 13,948 square miles) was the epicenter of the seven-hundred-year-old Mandinka Kingdom of Kaabu, which emerged after the collapse of the famous Mali Empire founded by the legendary Sundiata Keita in the thirteenth century. From its capital Kansala, near the modern city of Gabu in Guinea-Bissau, the *mansas* (rulers) of Kaabu exercised influence

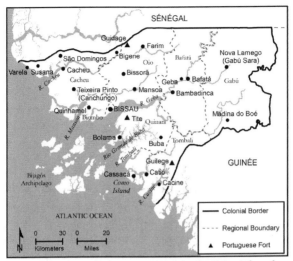

Map 1. Portuguese Guinea, ca. 1960. Map by Brian Edward Balsley, GISP.

northward to the south bank of the Gambia River and southward to parts of northern Guinea-Conakry. During the transatlantic slave trade, Kaabu was engaged in numerous military campaigns that secured captives for the plantations of the Americas. The kingdom collapsed in 1867 as a result of domestic political crisis and increasing external pressure from three ambitious European maritime powers: the British on the Gambia River, the French on the Casamance and Nunez Rivers, and the Portuguese on the network of waterways known as the Rivers of Guinea of Cape Verde.

The Portuguese were the first Europeans to reach Guinea-Bissau, with the landing of the explorer Alvaro

Fernandes in Varela in 1446. Ten years later, some of the islands of the Cabo Verde archipelago were "discovered" by two Genoese sailors in the service of Prince Henry the Navigator, Alvise Cadamosto and Antonio de Noli. Santiago and Fogo island were quickly settled by mainly Portuguese colonists and enslaved Africans from the adjacent coast. Claiming exclusive rights over her "lands of discoveries" in West Africa, Portugal was effectively challenged by her European rivals, resulting in her sphere of influence being reduced to the "Rivers of Guinea of Cape Verde"—roughly corresponding to coastal Guinea-Bissau. From this network of waterways, the voracious activities of illegal Cabo Verdean slave traders called *lançados* facilitated the shipment of millions of African captives to Cabo Verde and the Americas. The *lançados* also became the pioneers of Portugal's centuries-old entrenchment efforts in this area. In 1588, they founded one of the earliest Portuguese settlements on the West African mainland, the fortified town of Cacheu, in northwest Guinea-Bissau. Their attempts to undermine local sovereignties generated bloody conflicts. Nevertheless, over the centuries a constant flow of traders, missionaries, soldiers, colonial officials, and teachers from Cabo Verde continually descended on "Guinea of Cabo Verde," which became "Portuguese Guinea" in 1879.

It was in search of gainful employment that Amílcar Cabral's mother and father, Iva Pinhel Évora and Juvenal António da Costa Cabral, found themselves in Portuguese Guinea during the early decades of the twentieth century. Iva was born on 31 December 1893, the daughter of Maximiana Monteiro da Rocha and António Pinhel Évora, both of modest social backgrounds. She arrived in Portuguese Guinea in 1922 with her nine-month-old son, Ivo Carvalho Silva, and the baby's father, João Carvalho Silva. Shortly afterwards, she and her son separated from João, who had become a minor colonial official in Bolama, the capital of a "possession" hastily proclaimed on 18 March 1879 but yet to be "effectively occupied." Relocating to Bafatá around 1923, Iva met Juvenal Cabral, a primary school teacher in the nearby town of Geba.

The relationship between Iva and Juvenal produced four offspring: Amílcar, the twins Armanda and Arminda, and António. It lasted until 1929, during which time Amílcar lived two years in Bafatá without his father and three years in Geba with both parents.[1] Toward the end of 1929, Iva returned to Santiago, where, on Christmas Eve that year, Amílcar and his twin sisters were baptized at the Catholic Church of Nossa Senhora da Graça (Our Lady of Grace) in Praia, the capital of Cabo Verde.[2] Although she had intended to stay permanently, Iva was obliged to return with her children to Portuguese Guinea less than two years later due to difficulties in securing the basic needs of her family. They lived in Bissau, where Juvenal Cabral, recently married to Adelina Rodrigues Correia de Almeida (future mother of Luís Cabral), also resided. In 1932, Amílcar and his twin sisters returned to Cabo Verde with their father. Iva followed a year or so later and resumed care of her children.

Juvenal Cabral was born on 2 January 1889, the son of Rufina Lopes Cabral, of humble origins, and António Lopes da Costa, a final-year student at the São José Seminary on the island of São Nicolau who was from a notable landowning family in Santiago. Juvenal's paternal grandfather, Pedro Lopes da Costa, was one of the few Cabo Verdeans who "seriously cared about the education of children," such that his family produced "distinguished priests, teachers and civil servants" who "served well and honored well" the *patria* (fatherland) of Portugal.[3] With his father killed when Juvenal was only ten months old, the boy became the ward of his paternal grandfather Pedro and great-aunt Paula Lopes da Costa, and later his godmother, Simoa dos Reis Borges. Simoa inherited property upon the death of her brother in 1894, rented it, and four years later left for Portugal with her husband and eight-year-old godchild.

Juvenal Cabral attended primary school in Santiago de Cassurães, Beira Alta, Portugal, as the only black student "among forty young white boys." Upon graduation he entered the nearby Catholic seminary in Viseu, where one of his contemporaries was António de Oliveira Salazar, later to become the architect and dictator of the Estado Novo established in the aftermath of the 1926 military coup d'état that ended sixteen years of liberal democracy in Portugal. In 1905, due to financial difficulties, Juvenal was forced to abandon the seminary and return to Cabo Verde. Still determined to become a priest, he entered the seminary in São Nicolau, but once again his ecclesiastical studies were short-lived, lasting about a year, due to a disciplinary action against him for fighting with a student from Portuguese Guinea. Rather than endure "shame for being punished, like a child," he quit the seminary and returned to Santiago in July 1907.[4] Four years later, after a brief stay in Praia, he embarked for Portuguese Guinea "in search of employment, through the rewards of which I can decently maintain myself."[5] It was at the end of the first decade of a new century that had been inaugurated in Cabo Verde by a severe drought (1900–1903) that killed sixteen thousand people, a tragedy an angry contemporary Cabo Verdean lawyer, Luiz Loff de Vasconcellos, denounced as "a perfect extermination of a people," blaming Portugal for a "tremendous and horrific catastrophe" that the Lisbon authorities had dismissed with the callous excuse that "the government is not culpable that in Cabo Verde there have not been regular rains."[6]

The "voluntary" emigration of Amílcar's father and mother to Portuguese Guinea, in contrast to the "forced" exodus of Cabo Verdeans as *contratados* (contracted workers) to the notorious cacao plantations of São Tomé and Príncipe, occurred against the background of dire conditions in the archipelago. For more than three centuries, droughts and famines had regularly visited Cabo Verde, often lasting two to three years and causing spectacular death tolls, sometimes amounting to two-thirds of the inhabitants of some islands and up to half the population of the archipelago. These catastrophic natural and man-made disasters, together with brutal colonial exploitation and neglect, underlie the significant movements of the population, particularly during the second half of the nineteenth and first half of the twentieth centuries. Between 1902 and 1922, a total of 24,329 desperate Cabo Verdeans found themselves forced to become contracted migrant laborers, 98.5 percent ending up in São Tomé and Príncipe.[7] On the other hand, during the period 1900–1920 an estimated 27,765 Cabo Verdeans "voluntarily" migrated, mainly to the United States (67 percent), Portuguese Guinea (8 percent), Brazil/Latin America (7 percent), and Senegal/Gambia (5 percent). The "voluntary" flow to the United States was effectively restricted in 1917, when a new immigration law required, among other things, literacy. Obviously, the prolonged harsh realities in the face of neglect and exploitation render redundant the categorization of migration from Cabo Verde as either forced or voluntary. Both were motivated by the specter of starvation and death.

The relatively high literacy rate in Cabo Verde (22 percent in 1950) provided Portugal with a reservoir of willing collaborators—a collaboration conditioned by the prevalent poverty and limited employment opportunities. With a seminary established in 1866, a secular high school opened in 1917 (the first in Portuguese

Africa), and several primary schools, Cabo Verdeans were indeed the main beneficiaries of Portuguese colonial education. This factor largely accounted for their significant presence in the colonial administration of Portuguese Guinea—about 75 percent of the colonial officials before the beginning of the armed struggle. Such preponderance gave rise to their pseudo-status as "co-colonizers" or "proxy colonizers," notwithstanding the fact that Cabo Verde was a colony and Cabo Verdeans a colonized people with a history of brutal exploitation and callous abandonment to recurrent droughts and famines. With the Cabo Verdeans arbitrarily classified as *civilizados* (civilized), the colonial authorities endeavored to ensure that "to Guiné go only those with literacy skills who are going to fill public and business appointments."[8] For poor Cabo Verdeans, the main attraction to Portuguese Guinea was the territory's reliable agriculture and enhanced food security. As one Cabo Verdean writer and colonial official noted, the colony was the "blessed land of rice and nuts and palm oil, where hunger is unknown and there are no beggars."[9]

Portuguese Guinea was (and remains) a multiethnic and multicultural country inhabited by Balantas and Biafadas, Brames and Bijagós, Fulas and Felupes, Mandinkas and Manjacos, Pepels, Nalus, Susus, and several other minor groups that, altogether, have more in common than the sum total of their differences. Desperate to establish the *pax lusitana*, the Portuguese exploited the differences of language and culture and played off

31

one group against the other, constantly making a distinction between the Islamized "neo-Sudanese" Fulas and Mandinkas of the interior, the "builders of strong states," and the "animist paleo-Sudanese" of the coastal region, the "more backward peoples."[10] Applying a racist anthropology, colonial officials-cum-social scientists considered the neo-Sudanese to be of Hamitic/Semitic racial origins, which supposedly made them superior to all the other groups regarded as paleo-Sudanese. This strategy of divide and conquer would constitute a formidable challenge facing Amílcar Cabral as he and his comrades embarked on mobilizing the people for the armed struggle against Portuguese colonial domination.

Juvenal Cabral first worked as a clerk at the Bolama city hall, followed by two other low-level clerical positions in the colony's treasury department and the office of the secretary-general of the colonial government. In January 1913, he became a primary school teacher in Cacine, in the southern region of Tombali, where he taught half a dozen children in a one-room school. He also taught in Buba, Bambadinca, Bafatá, and Geba. Forming the background to his teaching trajectory were the brutal "pacification" campaigns waged by Captain Teixeira Pinto's mercenary soldiers, led by Senegalese warlord Abdul Injai. Juvenal supported the war against the Pepels of Bissau in 1915 and regarded Captain Pinto as "a great Portuguese" whose "patriotic work" was for "the good of civilization."[11] Such sentiment outraged the members of the Liga Guineense (Guinean League), founded on 25 December 1910 as "an assembly of the natives of Guinea." Reacting to the antiwar position of the Liga, the colonial authorities dissolved the emergent protonationalist organization in 1915.

The wanton brutality meted out to the Pepels of Biombo, one of the petty kingdoms on the island then known as Bissau, resulted in thousands of deaths and the capture of hundreds of fighters, including the ruler, N'Kanande Ká. Defiant in captivity, the king reportedly told Teixeira Pinto that he would never surrender, that as long as he was alive he would always fight to expel the Portuguese from his realm, and that "if he should die, and there in the other world he should meet whites, he would wage war on them."[12] Captain Pinto proudly reported that the Pepel king was promptly condemned to death, then "tied up, mutilated, his eyes plucked out, and buried alive." Luiz Loff de Vasconcellos, the outraged defense lawyer of the victims of the Bissau war, pointed out that after the defeat of the Pepels "the real carnage started," as "men, women, old people, children, and the crippled" were "mercilessly killed," their dwellings sacked and burned and their livestock looted, resulting in their homeland being "in the greatest desolation and misery."[13] That was just nine years before Amílcar Cabral was born. It would take two more brutal pacification campaigns, in 1925 and 1936, to subjugate the last resisters, the people of the Bijagós Islands.

Thus, when Cabral was born, Portuguese Guinea was simultaneously undergoing a brutal war of conquest and the consolidation of colonial domination by a weak imperial power that itself was experiencing tumultuous political upheavals following a bloody revolution that abolished the monarchy in 1910 and established a liberal republic, which was overthrown sixteen years later. In 1932, when eight-year-old Amílcar moved to Cabo Verde, António de Oliveira Salazar became prime minister of Portugal. As the effective dictator of the established New State he would maintain a brutal, repressive regime in the African colonies until his incapacitation by a stroke thirty-six years later. Cabral would devote his life to breaking the stranglehold of this harsh colonial order on the lives of the millions of Africans it subjugated.

Meanwhile, in Bafatá, two years before his son Amílcar was born, Juvenal made a passionate plea to the visiting governor for the provision of more schools for the natives, who were "still wrapped up in the plain cloak of their primitive ignorance."[14] Juvenal was indeed an outspoken advocate of the expansion of education in the territory, pleading strongly in 1915 for "the light of education to be shed on this people so desirous of lights" and insisting that, "as is already proven, the *gentio* is not devoid of intelligence, needing on our part to know only how to encourage him to love education."[15] His son Amílcar would inherit such passion for education, but as a weapon for liberation, "to combat fear and ignorance, to stamp out little by little submissiveness before nature and natural forces."[16]

When Amílcar was born, his father registered his first name as Hamilcar, to honor the great Carthaginian general whose son Hannibal was also a famous general. Bafatá was then a relatively new settlement, elevated to the status of a town in 1917, but would soon after become the second most important trading center (after Bissau) in the territory. Of the population of about 1,500 residents, half were Europeans, Lebanese, Syrians, and numerous *civilizados*—mostly Cabo Verdeans. The local economy was dominated by the production of export crops such as peanuts, cotton, and rubber, which were exported to Portugal and France by Portuguese and French trading companies including the Union Manufacturing Company (CUF), Casa Gouveia, Barbosa e Comandita Limitada, and the French West Africa Company (CFAO).

Notwithstanding his strong emotional and spiritual attachment to Cabo Verde and Portugal, Juvenal nevertheless recognized Portuguese Guinea as "the land where the genealogical tree of my ancestors grew and flourished," and declared that since his youth he had struggled for the "dignification of the black race to which I belong."[17] This firm identification with Portuguese Guinea and his ready recognition of his black African ancestry undoubtedly had an influence on his offspring, particularly Amílcar and his brother Luís Severino de Almeida Cabral (born in Bissau on 10 April 1931), who would later embrace their dualities of birthplace and ancestral home and subsequently adopt binationalism as a strategy for the liberation of their two countries.

In November 1932, Juvenal retired to Santiago, taking with him Amílcar and his twin sisters. Iva stayed in Bissau to recover the loss she suffered from a burglary, returning a year later to take custody of her children. Thus, Amílcar Cabral only spent about seven years in Portuguese Guinea before returning, for the second time, to Cabo Verde. Very little is known about his life during those tender years he lived in his *terra natal.* Neither he nor his father—whose autobiography, *Memorias e reflexões* (Memories and reflections), was written when Amílcar was a second-year agronomy student in Portugal—has left any written account of those early formative years.

Amílcar was conscious of the hard life his mother had, of the long hours she had to work to ensure that her four children did not go to bed hungry. The sacrifices, which grew bigger as the children became young adults, and especially in order for Amílcar to complete his high school education in Cabo Verde, would be appreciated by a grateful son. Amílcar would later express his gratitude by describing his mother in a dedicatory poem as "the star of my infancy," with the acknowledgment, "Without you, I am nobody."[18]

Thus, notwithstanding the affirmations of Cabral's notable biographers, particularly Mário de Andrade and Patrick Chabal, that Juvenal played a pivotal role in his son's development of critical political consciousness, it would appear that Iva was the central figure. The radical political consciousness of Amílcar fundamentally challenged his father's core political beliefs. Ironically, although Juvenal was a primary school teacher in Portuguese Guinea, Amílcar was not enrolled in any educational establishment in the territory, in spite of being of school age. It is probable that he was home-schooled, given the importance of education among Cabo Verdeans. Nevertheless, in Cabo Verde, Iva's determination for her children to be educated would be realized. Life in the archipelago would be critical in the molding of Amílcar's character.

Terra Ancestral

Schooling and Adolescence in
Cabo Verde, 1932–45

Late in November 1932, after an exhausting two-day boat trip from Portuguese Guinea, Amílcar Cabral and his five-year-old twin sisters Armanda and Arminda, accompanied by their father Juvenal Cabral, disembarked in Praia. For about two years the children lived with their father in the interior of Santiago, in his big house at Achada Falcão, near Assomada, capital of the municipality of Santa Catarina and the second-largest city on the largest island in Cabo Verde. The house was built on extensive land, shadowed by the Serra da Malagueta mountain range, that Juvenal inherited from his godmother, Simoa dos Reis Borges.

Mountainous with relatively fertile valleys, Santiago was also the first island to be settled, initially by Portuguese migrants from the regions of Alentejo and Algarve and the Madeira Islands, as well as a sprinkling of Genoese and Spaniards. The island quickly became the heartbeat of the archipelago. In 1466, the Portuguese

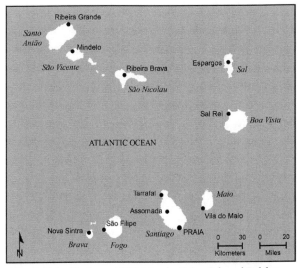

Map 2. Cabo Verde, ca. 1960. Map by Brian Edward Balsley, GISP.

Crown granted the Santiago settlers special privileges to have their own administration and the right to trade on the adjacent West African coast. Six years later, a royal decree gave them the right "to have slaves, males and females, for their services, and to be occasion for their better livelihood and good settlement."[1] But they were prohibited from trading in African captives, and for their defiance they became known as *lançados* (from the Portuguese word *lançar*—"to launch"—meaning those who defiantly "launched" themselves onto the West African mainland), with the Rivers of Guinea of Cabo Verde as their principal area of activity.

The enslaved Africans in Santiago and the other islands constructed the foundations of the new slave-based society with blood, sweat, and great toil. Theirs was a precarious existence that has been described as "hard, brutish and, in times of famine, short."[2] They worked the sugar and cotton plantations, gathered the vegetable dyestuff *urzela* and the oil-producing nut *purgueira*, wove the highly esteemed cotton cloths called *panos*, and extracted salt, besides a host of other tasks. Furthermore, the enslaved African women were sexually exploited by their masters, which resulted in the creation of a *mestiço* (mixed-race) racial category that became, through paternal inheritance, a dominant landowning class occupying important positions in the social and political life of the archipelago. The tendency of Portuguese men in the tropics to "unashamedly" have sexual relations with enslaved and "free women of color" would later be conceptualized by Brazilian sociologist Gilberto Freyre as "lusotropicalism," which theory equates "racial harmony" in the "world created by the Portuguese" with miscegenation. The Lisbon authorities would weaponize the concept to maintain the *pax lusitana*. Amílcar Cabral would dismiss Freyre as "confusing realities that are biological and necessary with realities that are socioeconomic and historical."[3]

With recurring drought and famine, decline in the transshipment of African captives to the Americas, and the emigration of numerous white settlers, Cabo Verde became a penal colony where Portugal sent her convicts, known as *degredados*. Miscegenation increased substantially during the period 1802–82, when some 2,433 convicts (among them 81 women) were deported to the islands, with Santiago receiving the majority of them.[4] This island would later host a concentration camp built by the Estado Novo in the town of Tarrafal in 1936, where Portugal sent her political dissidents and African nationalist agitators. By 1900, *mestiços* constituted 64 percent of the archipelago's population, among them the rich, the poor, and the marginalized. The "whites" made up 3 percent of the inhabitants, while the "blacks" accounted for the remaining one-third.

Invariably characterized as *brancos* (whites), *mestiços*, and *pretos* (blacks), the population of Cabo Verde had, from the beginning of slavery to the end of the colonial period, also been a race- and color-conscious society. While these socially constructed categories may never have been fiery, contentious issues, the absence of overt racial conflict did not mean the absence of either race/color consciousness or racial prejudice. Historically, race and color have had social, cultural, and psychological significance in the archipelago. From the early days of settlement, the *mestiço* element was differentiated from the black population and generally given favored treatment. The sons and daughters of white men, or their descendants, they generally considered themselves "white, Portuguese, and civilized," naturally superior to the blacks, and thus remained spiritually and psychologically amputated from Africa. Cabral

41

would take issue with such self-perception, admonishing that "some, forgetting or ignoring how the people of Cape Verde were formed, think that Cape Verde is not Africa because it has many *mestiços*," and insisting that "even if in Cabo Verde there was a majority white native population . . . Cape Verdeans would not stop being Africans."[5]

At home in Achada Falcão, Cabral found himself once again among a people with a long tradition of resistance against brutal exploitation and oppression. The municipality of Santa Catarina had been the epicenter of revolts and rebellions by a people referred to as *badius*, the poor black and *mestiço* peasants of the island.[6] Twenty-two years earlier, just a month after the Portuguese monarchy was overthrown and a republic declared (5 October 1910), the tenant farmers of Ribeirão Manuel revolted against the payment of rents, during a time of drought and famine, to the landowners known as *morgados*—a throwback to the latifundia-type system that emerged with the royal land grants of the early settlement period. The brutal response of the colonial authorities to the initial protests ignited a rebellion led by Nha Ana Veiga, popularly known as Nha'Ana Bombolom,[7] who rallied the angry peasants with her legendary call to arms: "homi faca, mudjer matxado, mosinhos tudo ta djunta pedra" (men knives, women machetes, all children gather stones).[8] According to Pedro Martins, a native of Santa Catarina and maternal relative of Cabral who, as a politically active high school

42

student six decades after the Ribeirão Manuel rebellion became the youngest political prisoner in the notorious Tarrafal concentration camp, the defeated leaders were "handcuffed" and "paraded around the island"—much like Gungunhana, the defiant ruler of the Gaza kingdom in southern Mozambique, who was defeated by the Portuguese in 1895, was taken to Portugal and paraded through the streets of Lisbon.

The Ribeirão Manuel revolt was preceded by uprisings in Ribeira de Engenhos in January 1822 and Achada Falcão in January 1841, both motivated by high rents and a highly exploitative land-tenure system dominated by a handful of mostly absentee landlords. The dependence of the majority of Cabo Verdeans on eking out a precarious living from an agriculture conditioned by soil erosion and cyclical droughts would later influence the decision of Cabral to study agronomy.

The struggles of poor peasant farmers in Cabo Verde were paralleled by those of urban workers, especially during the last quarter of the nineteenth and the first two decades of the twentieth centuries when the number of strikes and demonstrations increased in Mindelo, capital of São Vincente Island, where workers at the port, the coaling stations, and the shipping agencies demanded better wages and working conditions.

Resistance in the context of periodic droughts and famines has been a salient feature of the history of Cabo Verde, a history that is also embedded in the various facets of Cabo Verdean culture, including folklore, music, song, and dance. Young Amílcar, like most young Cabo Verdeans, was conscious of this sad trajectory of his ancestral country, but as an adult he would change such static consciousness to active engagement in social transformation, thus reconciling memory and action. As in the case of Portuguese Guinea, Amílcar would later regard the numerous revolts during slavery and the many acts of defiance in the colonial period as sources of inspiration for his anticolonial activism.

Life in Achada Falcão for Amílcar and his sisters was but short-lived, less than two years. Little is known about this brief period when Amílcar intimately lived part of his age of innocence with his father. The family house was big, made of brick with red roof tiles imported from Portugal. The air of opulence it exuded was reinforced by Juvenal's "proverbial generosity" in the face of ubiquitous poverty and misery, a generosity that included "lending money without guarantees."[9] With the severe drought and deadly famine of the early 1940s, having borrowed money against his property as collateral, Juvenal was forced to vacate the house and move with his family to Praia. Amílcar and his sisters had already moved out, when their mother finally reassumed responsibility for them shortly after her return from Portuguese Guinea in late 1933 or early 1934.

In Praia, Amílcar was enrolled at the Escolar Primária Oliveira Salazar, with his mother bearing the full cost of his upkeep and education.[10] During this period the city was under enormous stress due to a slump in agricultural and commercial activities in Santiago and the other islands, a significant rural urban migration provoked by cyclical droughts and famines, the perennial neglect of Portuguese colonial rule, and a world at war. A safety valve for the accumulating socioeconomic crisis was the increased recruitment of *contratados* for the cacao plantations of São Tomé and Príncipe. When two devastating famines (1941–43 and 1947–48) lasting five years officially killed 45,000 people (25 percent of the population), some 18,513 *contratados*, mostly poor *badius* from Santiago, "involuntarily" migrated south, mainly to São Tomé and Príncipe, while 6,898 more fortunate Cabo Verdeans "voluntarily" emigrated to Portugal (68 percent), Portuguese Guinea (20 percent), and the United States of America (5 percent).[11] Young Amílcar lived through the generalized hardships prevalent in the archipelago, where he "saw folk die of hunger" and witnessed the forced migration of "thousands . . . as contracted workers for the Portuguese plantations in other colonies," an experience that later left him sufficiently revolted and determined to struggle for the end of Portugal's colonial rule in Africa.[12]

At primary school, and later in high school, Cabral followed the same curricula as that of students in Portugal, since Cabo Verde was officially considered a "civilized" colony that was sufficiently assimilated to Portuguese culture, unlike the "uncivilized" mainland territories of Portuguese Guinea, Angola, and Mozambique. The educational system was broadly Eurocentric and narrowly Lusocentric, which meant total neglect of African history and culture. The education emphasized the learning of Portuguese language and culture and, besides basic mathematics and science, the celebration of the maritime "discoveries" of the fifteenth and sixteenth centuries, the "genius" of the "Father of Portuguese Literature," Luís de Camões, the miracles of Nossa Senhora de Fatima (Our Lady of Fatima), and the "historical mission" of Portugal. As a graduate of this paternalistic education, Cabral later scathingly commented on its racist content and alienating impact.

> All Portuguese education disparages the African, his culture and civilization. African languages are forbidden in schools. The white man is always presented as a superior being and the African as an inferior. The colonial "conquistadores" are shown as saints and heroes. As soon as African children enter elementary schools, they develop an inferiority complex. They learn to fear the white man and to feel ashamed of being Africans. African geography, history and culture are either ignored or distorted, and children are forced to study Portuguese geography and history.[13]

Thus, in such Eurocentric education, just as the children of the *assimilés* in France d'Outre-mer (Overseas France) were forced to recite "our forefathers the Gauls," so, too, young Amílcar found himself obliged to read "who are we, the Portuguese who for many centuries have lived in this corner of Europe? History says that we are the descendants of many ancient peoples who intermixed and intermingled."[14] He would retrospectively acknowledge the effectiveness of this colonial socialization process: "There was a time in my life when I was convinced that I was Portuguese." But he would also later realize that he was not Portuguese because of his consciousness of "my people, the history of Africa, even the color of my skin."[15] Such awareness was premised on the strong conviction that "the culture of the people of Cabo Verde is quintessentially African."[16]

In July 1937, Cabral graduated from primary school at the top of his class and passed his high school entrance examination with distinction. Together with his mother and siblings, he moved to Mindelo, São Vincente, and became one of the 372 enrolled students at the Liceu Infante Dom Henrique during the academic year that started on 21 October 1937. At age thirteen, he was two years older than the average enrolled first-year high school student. Five days after his enrollment (for courses that included Portuguese and French languages, mathematics, science, art, and physical education), the high school was closed by order of the minister of the colonies, Francisco Vieira Machado, who requested its transformation into a vocational school. The closure provoked strong protests from the enrolled students, who were supported by their families and the general public, resulting in the reopening of the school three months later as the Liceu Gil Eannes. A participant in the demonstrations, the effectiveness of organized protest left an enduring impression on young Amíl-car, a valuable learning experience and useful teachable moment that he would invoke three decades later in a seminar for the cadres of the PAIGC, pointing out, "I waited three months without going to classes at secondary school, because they [the colonial authorities] had closed it. For them what they had done was enough, no more was needed. From then on only training centres for fishermen and carpenters. The population rose and protested, and the secondary school began operating once more."[17]

The seven years Cabral spent in Mindelo were, as in Praia, extended days and months of hardships and deprivations made bearable by the sacrifices of his mother and older half-brother Ivo, each of whom worked daily many hours for very little pay. Cabral's mother labored in the local fish cannery, earning fifty cents an hour, where she worked eight hours a day when fish was plentiful and only an hour a day when fish was scarce. To supplement her meager income, she also worked as a laundress for Portuguese soldiers stationed on the island, since, despite her old craft as seamstress, "she made nothing from sewing." Amílcar's brother Ivo, who trained as a carpenter, did all kinds of odd jobs to contribute toward the upkeep of the household. Cabral himself helped by tutoring primary school and fellow *liceu* students.

Yet, in spite of the austere conditions he endured with his family in Mindelo, Cabral remained focused on his schoolwork and strove to surpass his classmates in all subjects. He quickly displayed the initiative and determination for which he would become well known. As class president throughout his high school years, his charismatic leadership won him numerous friends and admirers at the same time as it developed and refined his interpersonal skills and negotiating capabilities. The good impression he made on students and faculty lingered for years, as Manuel "Manecas" dos Santos, a later alumnus of the same high school and his comrade-in-arms in Portuguese Guinea, recalls.[18] Cabral was also involved in extracurricular activities in and around Mindelo, including the founding of a high school sports club, the Associação Desportiva do Liceu de Cabo Verde (Sports Association of the High School of Cabo Verde), of which he was not only president but also an active member, being an adept soccer player and a keen sportsman. The honing of his organizing and leadership skills would also include the staging and directing of plays for both high school students and the youth of Mindelo, plays in which he sometimes also performed as actor.

Cabral's extracurricular activities in Mindelo—where the Claridade literary movement, aimed at defining and affirming Cabo Verde's specific Crioulu identity, emerged a year or so before his arrival—also included the writing of poetry and prose. The Cabo Verdean identity that came to be known as Caboverdianidade had, as its organ of expression, the journal *Claridade: Revista de Arte e Letras*, which was first published in 1936 and last appeared (the ninth edition) in 1960. Led by Jorge Barbosa, Manuel Lopes, and Baltasar Lopes da Silva, the proponents of this concept came to be called the Claridosos. They initially set the tone for a nativist literature that focused on the existential crises generated by drought, famine, poverty, isolation, and migration. They did not challenge the colonial order, but instead framed the literary renaissance in a regional setting considered part of Western Europe rather than Western Africa.

Nevertheless, this new literature was a radical departure from the previous Eurocentric focus of the earlier poets and prose writers who were educated at the seminary in São Nicolau. Steeped in the Greco-Roman classics, these pre-Claridade literati were later criticized by Cabral for producing a literature in which "they forget the land and the people."[19] In particular, they composed poetry characterized by the themes of love, personal pain, exalted patriotism, and profound nostalgia. Some of the poems were written and/or translated into Crioulu and song as *morna*, the quintessential Cabo Verdean music and dance genre made famous worldwide by Cesária Évora (1941–2011), a native of Mindelo commemorated by the name of the international airport on São Vincente.

The main factors accounting for the emergence of the Claridosos generation include the archipelago's recurring drama of drought, famine, death, and emigration and the establishment of a secular coeducational high school with largely Cabo Verdean faculty and staff (unprecedented in Portuguese Africa) in Mindelo, the most cosmopolitan city in the archipelago, where the resident educated elite had easier access to foreign literature reflecting the perspectives of realism and impressionism as artistic movements. Significant also was the installation of the fascist Estado Novo and its increasingly suffocating stranglehold on the colonized and the stationing of a large number of Portuguese troops in the archipelago to bolster the defense of the colony. This increased military presence provoked clashes between the local inhabitants and racist white soldiers, which not only insulted the dignity of the Cabo Verdean people but laid bare the falsity of the assimilationist notion of equality between colonizer and colonized. Such developments generated a nativist awakening among the Cabo Verdean intellectuals that coalesced into the concept of Caboverdianidade, whose founders influenced Cabral's early endeavors in poetry and prose writing. He would later commend the Claridosos for having their "feet fixed to the ground" and realistically depicting Cabo Verde as a place "where the trees die of thirst, the men of hunger—and hope never dies."[20]

Thus it was with the outlook of the Claridosos that Cabral wrote his first poems, including "Chuva" (Rain), written in 1943, echoing the "drama of the rain." Cabral's early short stories included "Fidemar" (Son of the sea) and "Hoje e amanha" (Today and tomorrow), respectively written in 1942 and 1944. The first tells the story of a young man who is revolted by the dire conditions in the archipelago and agitates for change but decides to leave the islands and secure the wherewithal needed to make the necessary revolution; however, before he can return, the hero dies at sea during a naval battle. As noted by Chabal, the theme of this "poem of adolescence," as Cabral later characterized it, was not uncommon, being "representative of Cape Verde's sense of isolation from the rest of the world and the need to escape from this insular hell by seeking liberation outside."[21] In the second story, written during his final high school year but published five years later under the pseudonym Arlindo António when he was in the last year of his university studies in Lisbon, Cabral decries the evils of war and injustice, hatred and hardships, yet optimistically embraces a future with better prospects for a son he desires. Mário de Andrade notes that this essay represents "the first philosophical reflection of Amílcar" in which, with his desire for a son, he plans to reshape the future.[22]

While the poets and prose writers of *Claridade* were cultural nativists whose affirmation of Caboverdianidade did not challenge the fundamental premises of Portuguese colonialism, they were nevertheless not totally oblivious to developments in the rest of the African continent. For example, a poem by António da Silva Ramos titled "Abyssinia," which became a *morna* expressing outrage against the invasion of Ethiopia in October 1935 by Italian fascist dictator Benito Mussolini, reveals a rare Pan-African solidarity that urged Negusa Nagast (Amharic for "king of kings"; emperor) Haile Selassie, to defend his kingdom, "which is rightfully yours."[23]

The Claridade movement was later overshadowed by the radical Certeza generation of younger writers and poets who focused on the linkages between the dire conditions of the archipelago and its status as a colony, as well as the historical and cultural links between the islands and the adjacent African mainland. Thus, these literati sowed the seeds for the germination of political consciousness that would lead to nationalist activism. The few issues of the journal *Certeza* that first appeared in 1944 contained poems and prose whose messages were deemed sufficiently subversive by the vigilant International and State Defense Police (PIDE) to ban the publication a year or so later, even though the authors were not yet calling for the overthrow of the colonial status quo.

Although Cabral admired the Claridade and Certeza poets and writers, having recognized their critical role in the emergence of an archipelago-centric literature, he nevertheless criticized them for their limited vision. In a penetrating analysis of Cabo Verdean poetry written in 1952, he pointed out that the messages of the poets and writers had to transcend both "resignation" and "hope" and insisted that "insularity and droughts cannot justify endless stagnation." He further urged that "the escapist dream, the desire to leave, cannot remain the only theme," that a different dream should "no longer be a desire to depart but to create a new land inside our land."[24] It was a clarion call for profound transformational change. His radical political consciousness had crystallized in Portugal during the seven years he spent there as a student and a trained agronomist.

Cabral completed high school at the top of his class in 1944. His journey to Portugal occurred a year later, after he and his family moved back to Praia, where he obtained employment as a clerk in the government printing office. He successfully applied for a scholarship from the House of Students of the Empire (CEI) to study agronomy in Portugal.

Mãe Patria

Higher Education and Political Militancy in Portugal, 1945–52

Early in November 1945, Cabral disembarked in Lisbon, capital of the *mãe patria* (motherland), about a month after his classes had begun at the Higher Institute of Agronomy (ISA) of the Technical University of Lisbon. The late arrival was due to bureaucratic delays in processing his travel documents. The institute had admitted 220 applicants comprising twenty females and two hundred males, including Cabral, the only African student. The five-year course in agronomy was so rigorous and intensive that only twenty-five students proceeded to the third year; among them were Cabral and a female Portuguese student, Maria Helena de Ataíde Vilhena Rodrigues, his future wife.

Cabral excelled in his studies at the ISA, earning top grades in all his subjects and gaining respect and admiration not only from his peers and professors but also from the rector of the institute, who asked him to tutor his children. Yet, notwithstanding his demonstrated intelligence, he remained humble and approachable. His whole university experience enabled him to refine his engaging personality and spirit of tolerance, which enhanced his organizational skills.

Besides his academic and professional training, the historical, political, and sociocultural contexts of Portugal and the dynamic background of the wider world provided the substance for young Cabral's formation of a critical consciousness. This would bring about the fundamental transformations he had to undergo for his self-liberation—profound changes that would serve as a prerequisite for his commitment to struggle for the liberation of his fellow colonized Africans in "Portuguese Africa."

When Cabral started his studies in Portugal, the twelve-year-old Estado Novo regime was still struggling to consolidate its imperial fiat. The fascist dictatorship was established in 1933 to arrest Portugal's decades-old economic decline, a state of affairs aggravated by political upheavals epitomized by the overthrowing of the monarchy, which was preceded by the assassination of King Carlos I and his heir-apparent Prince Luís Filipe on 1 February 1908. This bloody event was followed by the short and ineffectual reign of the assassinated monarch's second son, Manuel II, and the establishment of a precarious liberal republic on 5 October 1910, which was ushered in by a violent coup d'état that claimed over fifty lives. Portugal became the third country in Europe with a republican constitution, after France and

Switzerland. However, during the sixteen years of republican statehood, the country had political instability second to none in Western Europe: scores of political killings, numerous actual and attempted military coups d'état, several civil wars, eight presidents (with only one completing his constitutional term of office), thirty-eight prime ministers, and forty-five governments that lasted, on average, four months.

Having established her present-day borders in 1149 with the final expulsion of the Moslem conquerors who dominated much of the Iberian Peninsula since 711, and having defeated the huge Castilian invading army in the defining battle of Aljubarrota in 1385, Portugal became a powerful unified nation characterized by strong centralized government, political stability, and sociocultural homogeneity. Nationalist pride, bolstered by scientific knowledge and the innovations of the Renaissance, enabled the country to embark on "voyages of discovery" under the visionary leadership of Prince Henry "the Navigator" that had profound impacts around the world. Its vast seaborne empire in Africa, Asia, and South America briefly made the fiercely nationalistic nation the richest country in Europe and the first superpower of modern times. The strong Portuguese nationalism and patriotic fervor demonstrated throughout the centuries were celebrated in literature and folklore and taught in colonial schools as part of the process of "civilizing" the colonized. Yet it did not dawn on the Portuguese colonizers that their unrelenting determination to be free and independent could also be an inspiration to their colonial subjects, like Cabral, to stubbornly seek their own freedom and independence.

Increased fiscal and economic stability under Salazar as minister of finance (1926 and 1928–32) and prime minister (1932–68) enabled the significant improvement of Portugal's physical and social infrastructure, including the establishment of the Technical University of Lisbon in 1930. The science- and technology-based university and its agronomy school were created to address the needs of a predominantly agricultural country and its colonies, endowed with valuable natural resources. It was thus the most unlikely place to produce future political leaders, let alone radical anticolonial activists. Cabral would embrace the vision and mission of the institution but defy the expectation of political conformity.

Already well-steeped in Portuguese history, literature, and culture from his primary and high school education in Cabo Verde, with excellent oral and written command of the "language of Camões,"[1] Cabral arrived with a strong self-esteem that enabled him to withstand the preconceptions and prejudices of his white colleagues and professors, in spite of being legally "Portuguese." Thus, from the onset, Cabral felt at ease with himself and with academic life, unintimidated by the new environment in which he was the only black student among privileged white classmates and professors.

While Cabral was comfortable in his own skin, he still had to deal with racism and its manifold manifestations. In Portugal, as in Europe generally, an upsurge of racism in the nineteenth century was propelled by prominent philosophers, social scientists, and politicians, among others, following Charles Darwin's landmark publications, *On the Origin of Species* (1859) and *The Descent of Man* (1871). The central polemical thesis about the evolution of animal and plant life through natural selection quickly spawned a pseudoscience, Social Darwinism, which expounded the inherent superiority of the white man and his responsibility to the inherently "inferior" races.

Regarding the supposed racial and intellectual inferiority of Africans, the famous Portuguese writer and politician Joaquim Pedro de Oliveira Martins insisted in 1880 that education for Africans was "absurd not only in the light of History, but also in light of the mental capacity of these inferior races." Contemptuous of Portugal's proclaimed double mission of civilizing and evangelizing the "inferior races" and "barbarous peoples" of Africa "placed between man and the anthropoid," Oliveira Martins sneered, "Why not teach the Bible to the gorilla and the orangutan, who have ears even though they cannot speak, and must understand, almost as much as the black, the metaphysics of the incarnation of the Word and the dogma of the Trinity?"[2]

The new generation of passionate *colonialistas* of the late nineteenth century also included António José

Enes (royal commissioner of Mozambique, 1891–95), who considered the African "a big child" and "half savage";[3] Mouzinho de Albuquerque (conquistador of Mozambique, 1895), who insisted that, in order "to educate and civilize the native," it was imperative "to develop in a practical way his aptitude for manual labor";[4] and Eduardo da Costa (governor-general of Angola, 1906–7), who warned about "the gross and dangerous error of considering equal, before the law, the civilized European and the savage inhabitant of the African bush."[5] It was the racist ideas of such staunch imperialists that came to form the cornerstone of Portuguese colonial philosophy and, during the Estado Novo era, became camouflaged with Gilberto Freyre's imaginary tale of "lusotropicalism."

Portuguese imperial triumphalism and hubris were hugely displayed at the three-month Colonial Exposition of Porto inaugurated on 16 June 1934, eleven years before Cabral arrived in Lisbon. Inspired by the London Exposition of the British Empire in 1924 and the International Colonial Exposition of Paris in 1931, this celebration of white supremacy was complete with exhibitions of reconstructed African villages showing the "exotic natives," who supposedly represented, in the words of British poet Rudyard Kipling, the "new-caught, sullen peoples, half-devil and half-child." The exposition was evidence of Portugal taking up Kipling's "White Man's burden." At Porto, the exhibition of sixty-three *pretos da Guiné* (blacks of Guinea) drew huge crowds of spectators who gaped and gawked at the half-naked "savage" women with their exposed breasts, the scantily clad men, and the nude children. The exotic Africans on display also included Angolans and Mozambicans in their replicated "natural habitats" of "primitive" mud-hut villages, in which they were required to live and display their putative lifestyles and cultures for the duration of the exposition. On show in much the same way as the animals in the nearby Porto zoo, the human exhibits were meant to testify to the supposed superiority of the white race. This was also the objective of the many expositions of the other European and American colonial powers during the nineteenth and twentieth centuries.

Thus, when Cabral arrived in Portugal, memories of the human zoo that characterized the Colonial Exposition of Porto were still fresh in the country. Five years earlier, an even bigger celebration of imperial pomposity, the Exposition of the Portuguese World, had been held in Lisbon (June–December 1940), calculated to promote the Estado Novo dictatorship, celebrate the consolidation of Portuguese sovereignty in the overseas provinces, and further reinforce the notion of white superiority.

While Cabral was very much admired by his white colleagues for his intellectual prowess, he nevertheless encountered overt racism within and outside the ISA. But he was psychologically and emotionally prepared. On the eve of his departure from Cabo Verde, his father talked to him about his own experience in Portugal four decades earlier. Juvenal described his stay in the metropole as the happiest years of his adolescence, although "very hard." He accordingly warned his son thus: "It is obvious that in the metropole you will not encounter racism so rooted as, let's say, in the United States. However, even in Lisbon, there can be manifestations of this abominable phenomenon. Do not be astonished nor lose your head, if you note among your future colleagues a certain attitude of reserve in relation to you." Alluding to the possible racial bias of his teachers in Portugal, Juvenal advised his son to always remember that "you must show knowledge more profound than any candidate of Portuguese descent," because, "taking into account your origin, your knowledge will be evaluated with greater rigor."[6] Already a brilliant elementary and high school student, Amílcar would have no problem heeding his father's advice.

Cabral's colleague and girlfriend, Maria Helena Rodrigues, a native of Chaves in northern Portugal, recalled the cold reception he received when she took him home to meet her family. "The adults in the village would not talk to him, only behind his back." But Cabral remained unruffled when the children of the village, who had never seen a black person, ran after him "to see and touch him," a spectacle which he accommodated by "letting them touch his head" and using the occasion as a teaching moment. "He explained to them where he came from, what Africa was and who the Africans were.

62

He explained to them that despite colour differences all men were equal."[7]

Walking around the ISA campus with Maria Helena, Cabral was "on numerous occasions . . . insulted for being with a white woman."[8] Again Cabral would remain composed and explain away the racist behavior as ignorance and lack of education. Yet he was aware that racism was not entirely due to lack of enlightenment, but rather a phenomenon embedded in Portuguese and European culture that permeated societies and institutions. His self-confidence remained intact and enabled him to teach Portuguese adults in the poor working-class Lisbon neighborhood of Alcântara.

Cabral's arrival in Portugal occurred two months after the formal surrender of Japan on 2 September 1945, which signaled the final end of the Second World War and the dawning of an ideological rivalry between the two emergent superpowers, the United States and the USSR. Against the struggles of the Portuguese people for a democratic Portugal in the aftermath of the defeat of Nazi Germany and Fascist Italy, the Estado Novo dictatorship built a levee of authoritarian rule that effectively blocked the surging second wave of democratization that had begun to wash away entrenched dictatorships, including imperial overlordships, around the world. On the same day that Japan capitulated, the Vietnamese nationalist leader Ho Chi Minh declared the independence of the former French colony of Vietnam, thereby initiating the post-1945 decolonization process.

The fledgling Cold War that divided the world into two powerful blocs with military alliances to counterweigh and outmaneuver each other would be a favorable factor for decolonization.

Cabral's deepening political consciousness and subsequent political activism in Portugal were the result of his engagement in extracurricular self-education and participation in radical politics. At the ISA, he quickly became actively involved in radical student politics. According to Maria Helena, Cabral not only "participated actively in the student antifascist committees," but he also "led the discussions, since he expressed himself very well."[9]

Student opposition to the Estado Novo dictatorship was largely organized by the Movement of Democratic Unity (MUD), which had a youth section, the Youth Movement of Democratic Unity (MUDJ). Established in October 1945, MUD was a coalition of regime opponents that included communists, socialists, liberals, monarchists, labor unionists, and freemasons. The Portuguese Communist Party (PCP), founded in March 1921, was a very active member of MUD, through which it was able to disseminate Marxist-Leninist ideology that would influence Cabral and some of the other African students, including Agostinho Neto from Angola and Vasco Cabral (no relation of Amílcar) from Portuguese Guinea.

As a member of MUDJ, whose leadership included Mário Soares, the future leader of the Portuguese Socialist Party (PS) and president of post–Estado Novo

Portugal, Cabral got involved in electoral mobilization drives and spoke at meetings in which he also led and moderated some of the discussions. With increasing harassment and brutal repression by the International and State Defense Police (PIDE), most of the opposition boycotted the legislative elections, leaving Salazar's National Union party to retain its dominance in the Portuguese National Assembly and over political life in Portugal and her overseas provinces until its demise in 1974. Nevertheless, in spite of the tightening firm grip of the fascist regime, Cabral did not despair. Instead, the unfolding repressive situation strengthened his resolve and energized him to become more actively engaged in life-threatening political activities, as he pointed out in 1949: "I live life intensively and follow from it experiences that have given me a direction, a life I must follow, whatever personal sacrifices it asks of me."[10]

Cabral's intensive life as a politically active student in Lisbon revolved around his engagement in high-risk antiregime activities that were under the close surveillance of the PIDE. He continued to participate in political protests and demonstrations that put some of his African friends in jail, notably Vasco Cabral, Agostinho Neto, Mário de Andrade, and Marcelino dos Santos. Cabral was signatory to a petition to President Francisco Craveiro Lopes protesting Portugal's membership in NATO, which involved expenditure on weapons of war "while the Portuguese people live poorly." Antecedent to his anticolonial struggles, Cabral would gain valuable experience from such political militancy, which included practical experience of organizing clandestine activities in a repressive environment. He would later reference his active involvement in the antifascist struggle of the Portuguese people as his "loyalty" to Portugal "without being Portuguese."[11]

The political activism of Cabral in Lisbon also involved participation in the activities of the Casa dos Estudantes do Império (House of Students of the Empire; CEI), where students from the Portuguese empire congregated and socialized. The Casa was established by the Estado Novo in October 1944, ostensibly as a social center, but fundamentally a means for effective control of potentially subversive student activism. Overseen by the ministry of the colonies, it was considered "indispensable" in the effort to "create among the students a more useful national mentality," in order to count on their "dedication, patriotism and goodwill."[12] Just as the youth of the metropole had to be controlled by creating the Mocidade Portuguesa (Portuguese Youth), a compulsory youth organization established in 1936, so too the potentially restless students from the empire had to be closely managed. Nevertheless, the CEI would fail to abort the birth of anticolonial radicalism, and Cabral would be among the first generation of CEI affiliates to return home and initiate the process of dismantling the Portuguese empire in Africa.

The CEI was a meeting place of two groups of African students: those with scholarships provided by the

Estado Novo and/or colonial authorities, and those whose educational expenses were met by their families—mostly the children of rich white and *mestiço* parents who constituted the economic, bureaucratic, and military elites of the colonies, the overwhelming majority of whom defended the colonial status quo. Cabral belonged to the much smaller group of *bolseiros* (scholarship holders) that also included Vasco Cabral, Agostinho Neto, Mário de Andrade, and Marcelino dos Santos. It was mainly these relatively less privileged African students who began to effectively and sustainably challenge the Portuguese imperial order in their homelands.

The CEI was a house organized along "sections," with Cabral serving as secretary (later vice president and president) of the section representing Cabo Verde, Portuguese Guinea, and São Tomé and Príncipe students. In 1950 he was elected as the secretary-general of the CEI and a year later as its vice president. Cabral was also president of the cultural committee and an active collaborator in the management and publication of the CEI's literary organ, *Mensagem* (Message).

At the CEI, Cabral learned about the realities of colonial rule in Portugal's other African colonies. His acquaintance with fellow African students and the camaraderie that ensued with a handful of them, including Marcelino dos Santos (his roommate), Mário Pinto de Andrade, and Agostinho Neto, facilitated the learning process. Access to radical literature on Marxism,

Negritude, and Pan-Africanism deepened Cabral's knowledge of historical social phenomena and broadened his worldview. Marxist ideology was absorbed from literature provided by the PCP as well as from his militancy in the MUDJ, while the ideas of Negritude and Pan-Africanism were grasped through enthusiastic reading of available published works, beginning with the landmark publication of Léopold Sédar Senghor's critically acclaimed *Anthologie de la nouvelle poésie nègre et malgache de langue française* (1948).

Founded by Léopold Senghor, Aimé Césaire, and Léon Damas, respectively from France's colonies of Senegal, Martinique, and French Guiana, Negritude was a literary movement against French cultural imperialism. It emerged in Paris during the decade before the Second World War, which witnessed the launching of two short-lived literary journals, *La revue du monde noir* (1931–32) and *Légitime défense* (1932), both of which published poems and articles that critically questioned France's policy of assimilation. In 1935, in collaboration with Senghor and Damas, Césaire founded *L'étudiant noir*, the maiden issue of which contained his article "Conscience raciale et révolution sociale" ("Racial Consciousness and Social Revolution"), in which the term "Negritude" was first used. In defiant rejection of assimilation to French and European culture, this equally short-lived journal that launched the Negritude movement broadened the base of attack on French and European imperialism to include the whole world. It thus celebrated African and diaspora African cultures. The cultural resistance was influenced to some extent by the eloquent expressions of the African American ordeal and the celebration of black culture in the United States, as reflected in the works of the Harlem Renaissance poets and writers including Claude McKay, Countee Cullen, Langston Hughes, and Zora Neale Hurston.

The impact of Senghor's *Anthologie* on the evolving cultural and political consciousness of Cabral is reflected in his excitement about the book, which revealed to him "things I had not dreamed of, marvelous poetry written by blacks from all parts of the French world, poetry that speaks of Africa, of slaves, of men, of life, and of the aspirations of men." Cabral further noted that "the book brings me much, including, among many things, the certainty that the black man is in the process of awakening throughout the world."[13]

Consequently, Cabral and the other African students similarly influenced by the central message of Negritude began to focus on addressing the issue of cultural alienation. Cabral would later recall that the quest for cultural identity entailed the "re-Africanization of the spirit," or a "return to the roots" through rediscovery and embracement of African cultural heritages. Accordingly, Cabral and his colleagues organized poetry-reading sessions and talks at the CEI that focused on African cultures and societies. Their Afro-centric writings, including Cabral's poems "Regressa" (Return) and "Rosa Preta" (Black rose) and his short

69

story, "Hoje e Amanhã" (Today and tomorrow), were mostly published in *Mensagem*.

This emergent group of "culturally liberated" African students that Mário de Andrade later called "the generation of Cabral," who read the same books, discussed the same issues and concerns, and closely followed developments in other parts of the world—including "the triumph of the Chinese Revolution, the success of the USSR, [and] what was happening in North America (we all read a book about the blacks of America)"—would later focus their attention and energy on the more dangerous question of the independence of their countries.[14] Hitherto, their political activism had been limited to engagement in the antifascist struggle of the Portuguese people. The shift also reflected a significant divergence between Cabral's group of radical African students and their "comrades" in the PCP and other antifascist organizations on the fundamental question of decolonization. Like their counterparts in France and other European metropoles, the Portuguese progressive forces at the time did not advocate the end of colonialism, nor did they question the racist assumptions of the policy of assimilation. For Cabral and his colleagues who imbibed the ideology of Marxism-Leninism, the anticolonial struggle trumped the proletarian revolution. The imperative was the complete dismantlement of a racist and exploitative colonial structure.

Although Cabral was aware that Negritude was not a political movement, he nevertheless realized that a colonized people could not be truly liberated until they had regained their cultural identity. Seven years into the armed struggle in Portuguese Guinea, he would re-emphasize this awareness during a lecture in the United States in honor of his assassinated comrade in arms, Eduardo Mondlane, which he delivered on 20 February 1970 at Syracuse University: "A people who free themselves from foreign domination will not be culturally free unless . . . they return to the upward path of their own cultures." Therefore, he concluded, "national liberation is necessarily an act of culture."[15]

What Cabral learned from his extracurricular education and political activism in Lisbon would inform his thoughts and actions even before he became an active liberation fighter. On vacation in Cabo Verde in the summer of 1949, when he briefly worked as a substitute broadcaster at the Radio Clube de Cabo Verde, he tried "to awaken Cabo Verdean public opinion against Portuguese colonialism" with his program called *A nossa cultura* (Our culture). In the broadcast, he outlined the links between the archipelago and the West African mainland and characterized Cabo Verdean culture as essentially African, thereby undermining the Portuguese claim that the colonized islanders represented the best example of successful assimilation to the culture of the colonizer. Correctly perceiving the announcement as nuanced criticism, Governor Garcia Alves Roçadas promptly banned the program and fired Cabral.

Nevertheless, Cabral was able to publish five articles on agronomy in the official newsletter *Cabo Verde:*

Boletim de propaganda e informação established by Roçadas. In his critical scientific studies titled "Some Considerations about the Rains" and "In Defense of the Land," Cabral not only diagnosed Cabo Verde's two-hundred-year crippling affliction, but also prescribed remedies that included the storage of rainwater, construction of dikes and dams, and reforestation.

Returning to Portugal, Cabral intensified his quest to "return to the roots" and learn more about Africa. With the CEI under closer surveillance by the PIDE, another venue for the "re-Africanization of the spirit" had to be found. The Center for African Studies (CEA) was housed at the home of a member of the generation of Cabral, Alda do Espírito Santo, a university student from São Tomé and Príncipe who was one of the few females who frequented the CEI. According to Mário de Andrade, the meeting place became "the center of our conversations about Africa: there we studied geography, history, literature, our languages, our political problems." Cabral was actively involved in the organization of the CEA's program of activities, mainly lectures and debates focused on themes including human geography, African society and economy, black identity, Portuguese colonialism, and the African diaspora.

On 21 October 1951, the first of the CEA's series of lectures, organized by Cabral, started with a presentation by Francisco José Tenreiro, a geographer from São Tomé and Príncipe, on the "Geographical Structure of the Continent and Anthropological Structures."

Cabral's lecture on "Cultivation Systems Characteristic of the Black African: Advantages and Disadvantages of the Itinerant System" followed a few weeks later. He had, in the previous year, successfully completed his agronomy coursework at the ISA with a dissertation titled "The Study of Erosion and Land Defense in the region of Cuba (Alentejo)," for which he conducted field studies in that Portuguese region. Other lecturers included Mário de Andrade, Agostinho Neto, and Noémia de Sousa, with presentations largely based on their areas of study.

The CEA thus became the forum where the generation of Cabral learned from each other's research and lived experiences, critically reexamined their own identities and values, and "interpreted the problems of Africa and of the Black world."[16] Collaboration with prominent black intellectuals based in Paris enabled Cabral and some of his CEA colleagues to publish their works in *Présence africaine*, the scholarly journal of the Negritude movement founded in 1947 by the Senegalese writer Alioune Diop. In a special edition of the journal published in 1953 and titled *Les étudiants africains parlent* (African students speak), Cabral contributed an article on "The Role of the African Student" in which he urged educated Africans to strive to serve the laboring masses of the continent who had "no voice to express their most elementary needs."[17]

On 20 December 1951, Cabral married Maria Helena Rodrigues in a simple civil ceremony in Lisbon attended by a few of their close friends. Two months later, having completed an internship at the National Agronomy Station in Santarem, he successfully defended his practicum dissertation titled "About the Concept of Soil Erosion," which earned him the outstanding grade of 18/20.

About a month after qualifying as a professional agronomist, Cabral received a telegram from his brother Luís in Cabo Verde informing him of the death of their father on 20 March 1952. Deeply grief-stricken, he went into self-imposed solitary confinement in his bedroom for several days.

In June 1952, Cabral the trained agronomist signed a three-year contract with the Overseas Ministry to work in the Agriculture and Forestry Services of his *terra natal*. Three months later, he boarded the passenger boat *Ana Mafalda* bound for Bissau, with stopovers in São Vincente and Praia. On 17 September, a day before arriving in São Vincente, he wrote a letter to his wife in Lisbon urging her to "pack up everything quickly and come," because "we have a lot to do and we shall accomplish something, if conditions permit."[18] In Praia, he reunited with his mother and siblings and committed to having them rejoin him in Bissau as soon as possible.

Cabral's sense of mission was reflected in the poem "O adeus à Tapada" (Farewell to Tapada), written at the completion of his studies at the ISA, which was located in the Lisbon neighborhood of Tapada. In it, he bade farewell to his "comrades" and acknowledged "the

weapon" with which "to struggle" that he had been provided by the Institute.

Thus, when Amílcar Cabral embarked for Portuguese Guinea, his heavy baggage also contained the
weapon of theory and valuable practical experience in
clandestine political activism.

4

Return to *Terra Natal*

Colonial Service and
Anticolonial Activities, 1952–56

Cabral disembarked in Bissau on 20 September 1952. Four days later, he wrote another letter to his wife describing his country of birth as one of "the most beautiful lands that I have seen." Imbued with excitement and optimism, he told her that the conditions in the colony were conducive to work and success that hinged on the "vivification of life."[1] Over the course of twenty-one years, Cabral's radical enlivening of spirits would effectively challenge the Portuguese colonial order and culminate in the declaration of the independence of his country, albeit at a high human cost that would include his life.

The year 1952 marked a critical turning point in the life of Cabral. It also witnessed landmark developments in Africa that would favorably facilitate the realization of what Maria Helena described as the great and consuming ambition of her husband: "to go to Guinea and engage in political work . . . to go back 'home' and fight there."[2]

Cabral's return to Portuguese Guinea occurred against the background of a gathering strong "wind of change" in Africa: the end of Italian rule in Libya in December 1951; a coup d'état in Egypt in July 1952 that toppled the British puppet King Farouk and declared the country an independent republic; declaration of a state of emergency in Kenya in October 1952 followed by the arrest and imprisonment of nationalist leaders, including Jomo Kenyatta, which rapidly escalated the armed struggle of the "Mau Mau" rebels (who called themselves the Land Freedom Army) and culminated in independence a decade later; and a series of anticolonial demonstrations and strikes in Morocco resulting in the massacre of several hundred unarmed civilians by the French in December 1952 and the exile of King Mohammed V, intensifying the struggle for independence, which was finally achieved four years later.

Closer to Portuguese Guinea, in the British colony of the Gold Coast, the successful nonviolent "positive action" campaign led by Kwame Nkrumah culminated in a landslide electoral victory in February 1951, his immediate release from a two-year prison sentence, and his appointment as leader of government business, leading to independence in March 1957. Convinced that independence was not only the manifest destiny of his country but also that of all the colonized territories of Africa, Nkrumah would hastily organize the All-African People's Conference in Accra on 8–13 December 1958, described as "a gathering of African Freedom Fighters

. . . for the purpose of planning the final assault upon imperialism and colonialism."[3] Cabral would be one of the over three hundred delegates who attended the landmark convocation that would resolve to provide "full support to all fighters for freedom in Africa."[4] His liberation movement would be a beneficiary of such Pan-African solidarity.

In the neighboring colony of Guinée Française (French Guinea), the decolonization process gathered momentum in 1952 when the labor union leader Ahmed Sékou Touré became the head of the Democratic Party of Guinea (PDG), the local branch of the African Democratic Rally (RDA)—the interterritorial political party of the French African colonies. The collision course with imperial France would climax six years later, when Sékou Touré and the PDG rejected the neo-colonial project of self-government within a proposed Union Française (French Union). The consequential "No" vote in the referendum of 28 September 1958 would lead to the declared independence of Guinée four days later, and this new nation would greatly facilitate the armed liberation struggle that would be waged by the PAIGC led by Cabral.

A day after his arrival in Bissau, Cabral reported for duty at the Pessubé Agricultural Experimental Station, located on the Granja (farm) in the outskirts of the capital, as *engenheiro agrónomo de segunda classe* (engineer agronomist, second class). He was the first Guinean agronomist. The following day, after lodging in a hotel for three days, he moved to his new home located in the Granja. Thereafter, he busied himself adjusting to his new work environment and the rhythms of colonial life.

The country that Cabral encountered in 1952 was significantly different from the one he left in 1932. In the intervening two decades, Portugal had finally completed her "pacification" of the territory and established "effective occupation." With the obsession of the Estado Novo to maintain the *pax lusitana* at all costs, the colony was inundated with repressive laws aimed at silencing dissent and curbing political activity. A year before Cabral had last left his *terra natal*, strict censorship of the colonial press was imposed, followed two months later by an ominous warning from the first Estado Novo governor that everyone in the colony was expected to "honor the Mother Country by submission to her designs, by respect for her institutions, by love for her venerable traditions."[5]

Prior to Cabral's return, anticolonial activities in Portuguese Guinea were very limited. Before 1950 there were no active political organizations in the territory demanding full independence or autonomy. Significantly, a supposed proto-nationalism had been nipped in the bud decades before, soon after its manifestation in the guise of the Guinean League. Misleadingly describing itself as "an assembly of the natives of Guinea," the League was in fact an assembly of a small group of relatively privileged individuals. The rank-and-file comprised "civilized" petty officials, small traders, and shopkeepers, concentrated mainly in Bissau and Bolama. On the other hand, the League's leadership consisted exclusively of educated Guineans and Cabo Verdeans who were committed to the Portuguese colonial venture. Membership did not extend to the overwhelming majority of "the natives of Guinea." Although it had no political ambitions, the League acquired political relevance through the attempts of colonial authorities to link it to the resistance of the *gentios* against the brutal "pacification" campaigns of the day. As noted earlier, the antiwar criticisms of its members, made from a humanitarian rather than an anticolonial stance, led to its disbandment in 1915.

Thus, dissent in Portuguese Guinea was effectively stifled at a much earlier stage. Unlike Angola and Mozambique, where the protests of the colonial elites were deeply rooted, with numerous forums for reformist/ assimilationist politics that lasted through more than three decades of official hostility, the colonial authorities in Portuguese Guinea successfully arrested the growth of incipient nationalism. But opposition to the colonial order continued in the form of passive resistance through which the voiceless masses manifested their discontent and hostility in various ways, from individual defiance against forced labor and the payment of taxes to mass emigration to the neighboring colonies of French Guinea, Senegal, and Gambia. Cabral would characterize this prelude to the armed struggle as a period "of silent repression, of secret recourse to violence, of unsung victims, of disorganized individual reaction, of assaults and crime of all sorts taking place within the four walls of the administrative buildings."[6]

It was in this colonial context that Cabral found himself in Portuguese Guinea. Nationalist agitation was incipient. A year before his return, the Lisbon authorities had tactically changed the nomenclature of their territories from "colonies" to "overseas provinces," in the vain hope of deflecting the growing anticolonial sentiment in such international forums as the United Nations. Aware of the strengthening windstorms gathering over her African colonies, Portugal vowed to withstand the impending wave of decolonization. With the Tarrafal concentration camp in Cabo Verde only a two-day boat trip away, the ruthless International and State Defense Police (PIDE) became active, with four agents in Bissau in the early 1950s. Cabral and his wife, together with other suspected "troublemakers," would be promptly placed under active surveillance. The Cabrals were soon reported to be comporting themselves "in a manner that raises suspicion of activities against our presence."[7] By 1959, the PIDE deployment would increase to thirty-five operatives, and its singular mission would remain the squelching of nationalist upsurge through imprisonment, torture, and assassination.

Nevertheless, to implement his political agenda, Cabral had to acquaint himself with a country and a people he barely knew. He had to start by learning about the realities of the *regime do indigenato*. He was already aware of the country being a divided land of the "civilized" and the "uncivilized," of the "assimilated" and the "heathens"—a color-conscious, compartmentalized universe of *brancos*, *mestiços*, and *pretos*. He understood that the Portuguese strategy of divide and rule had succeeded in creating a category of colonized people that "assimilates the colonizer's mentality, and regards itself as culturally superior to the people to which it belongs and whose cultural values it ignores or despises."[8] He distinguished between a petty bourgeoisie that was "heavily committed and compromised with colonialism" and a potentially revolutionary petty bourgeoisie that was nationalist.[9] Theorizing, he would insist that for the nationalist petty bourgeoisie to identify with and protect the interests of the peasants and wageworkers after the achievement of political independence, it would have to "commit suicide as a class." This would become one of his truly original ideas that still resonates in Africa today.[10]

According to the 1950 population census, the "assimilated" petty bourgeois class to which Cabral belonged numbered 8,320 individuals, or a mere 1.6 percent of the territory's inhabitants. Among them, 27 percent were "whites," 55 percent were "mixed-race" (the overwhelming majority of them Cabo Verdeans), and 18 percent were "blacks." Ironically, in spite of the stated importance of literacy and fluency in Portuguese for "civilized" status, the illiteracy rates among these three racial categories were respectively 24 percent, 51 percent, and 52 percent. Furthermore, among the literates, 27 percent had elementary schooling, 9 percent completed high school, and a miniscule 1.4 percent graduated from postsecondary (including vocational) institutions.[11] Indeed, on the eve of the armed liberation struggle, Portuguese Guinea would have only fourteen university graduates, including Amílcar Cabral.

Cabral's wife arrived in early November 1952 and started working as an agronomist with her husband at the Granja. Their first child, a girl they named Iva Maria, whom Cabral would fondly call "Mariva," was born five months later, in Bissau, on 23 April 1953. The family home in the Granja was an open house where the Cabrals often provided food to their low-level coworkers, besides organizing parties that Cabral would use as a ploy to discuss nationalist politics. Carmen Pereira, who followed her husband (recruited by Cabral) to war and later became the only woman in the twenty-four-member Executive Council of the Struggle (CEL), recalled attending such *festas*, at which Cabral and a small number of male guests would disappear into a locked room while the festivity continued uninterrupted.[12]

Among Cabral's early acquaintances in Bissau were some of the large number of Cabo Verdean colonial functionaries in the territory, including Aristides Pereira, a post office telegrapher, and Abilio Duarte, a bank official: both would become his close comrades in clandestine anticolonial activities. Cabral also knew some of the high-ranking Cabo Verdean officials who, suspecting his political aims, advised him to refrain from "matters" that would jeopardize his prestigious "career as an engineer." And Cabral would be reminded that, like them, he too was "Portuguese." He promptly dismissed these diehard colonialists as a lost cause, noting "there is no cure."[13]

Cabral got to know some of the Guinean nationalists like Rafael Barbosa, Fernando Fortes, and Elisée Turpin, future founding members of the African Independence Party (PAI), which later became the PAIGC. His associates also included some of the metropolitan Portuguese he broadly described as "the human instruments of the state." Among them were a few political exiles, including the pharmacist Sofia Pomba Guerra, the first antifascist woman activist imprisoned in Mozambique, in 1949, for attempting to establish a cell of the Portuguese Communist Party.[14] Released a year later, Sofia ended up in Bissau, where she opened a pharmacy and taught high school English at the same time as she recycled French and Portuguese communist literature to some of the local nationalists. She would introduce Aristides Pereira and other Cabo Verdean and Guinean activists to Cabral. Her pharmacy assistant Osvaldo Vieira would become a famous guerrilla commander in the PAIGC.

Importantly, Cabral needed to familiarize himself with the rural population that bore the brunt of colonial exploitation. His big break came almost a year later, when he was appointed by Governor Diogo Mello e Alvim to conduct an agricultural census, the first of its kind in not only Portuguese Guinea but the entire Portuguese empire in Africa. The survey was commissioned by the Ministry of Overseas Provinces in August 1953, in fulfillment of Portugal's commitment to the United Nations Food and Agriculture Organization six years earlier. For Cabral, it meant extensive travel and the opportunity to learn at first hand the realities of Portuguese colonial rule as experienced by the overwhelming majority of the people, knowledge of which was vital for a successful mobilization for anticolonial struggle.

From the onset, Cabral the agronomist and research director sought to invigorate the Pessubé agricultural station he had found in a state of "lethargy and abandonment" with activities that would address "the need for the existence of an agricultural experimental post whose objective should be the improvement of agriculture."[15] In an undisguised criticism of what had hitherto been the use of the station for the benefit of the Portuguese colonizers and their collaborating colonial elites, he insisted that Pessubé should not serve as the "granja of the State . . . to satisfy the vegetable and fruit needs of some inhabitants of the capital." Consequently, he urged that the research and experimental dimension of the station should be "scientifically oriented, in order to achieve immediate practical results that serve the progress of land and man." To test the seriousness of the colonial authorities, Cabral boldly challenged his superiors "to create the indispensable conditions for a real and useful activity" of the agricultural station—otherwise, he argued, "it is not worth nourishing any longer its fictitious existence." Methodical in approach and praxis, he created a *Boletim informativo* (Information bulletin) "to enunciate the works realized or in progress, as well as the difficulties encountered, the defeats suffered or the victories achieved."[16]

Agriculture was the base of the economy of Portuguese Guinea. The colonial economy was essentially a peasant economy, despite attempts during the early years of the *pax lusitana* to create a plantation economy. The remarkable expansion of commodity production (of peanuts, palm kernels, rubber, and rice) for export was achieved without any fundamental dislocation of indigenous institutions, without any major technological innovations, and without significant expropriation of land or displacement of the peasantry. In particular, the colonized Guineans were spared the brutal enforcement of harsh labor codes notorious in Angola, Mozambique, and São Tome and Príncipe. While the peasants engaged in the cultivation and gathering of export commodities were motivated by the obligation to pay colonial taxes, they were also driven by the need to acquire money to purchase goods and fulfill certain social obligations. Cabral's insistence that the raison d'être of the Pessubé station should be "the improvement and the progress of the Guinean economy" was also recognition of this colonial reality.

The census operations started on 22 September 1953, with Cabral using a sampling method for the survey and applying his scientific methodology of "studying, measuring and inquiring." With his wife Maria Helena (forestry engineer and codirector) and a team of about fifteen census takers trained by him, Cabral spent seven months crisscrossing the mainland and the offshore Bijagós archipelago to gather relevant information about land usage, crop cultivation, and soil conditions, among other tasks. Covering some 60,000 kilometers of travel to visit 356 settlements in 41 districts of the 11 administrative divisions of the territory, the census team surveyed 2,248 peasant family holdings (out of a total of 85,478). Completed in April 1954, the collected data was analyzed and the final report submitted to the governor in December that year. Cabral acknowledged "the understanding and good will manifested by the native farmers, whose civility greatly facilitated the surveys." Acknowledgement of the collaboration of the "uncivilized natives" was most unusual in the publications of colonial officials in Portuguese Guinea. Such gesture reflected Cabral's humanistic values.

Conducting the agricultural census enabled Cabral to gain important knowledge about the essential nature of the colonial economy and the people whose lives and livelihoods depended on it. It was valuable information that showed the exact locus and importance of the various groups in the colonial economy. The landmark study also provided strategic information to the colonial authorities, whose very presence was predicated on the thorough exploitation of the natural and human resources of the territory. Three decades earlier, Governor Velez Caroço blatantly stated that Portugal "should not try to develop Guinea simply to satisfy her own need," but, instead, should "ensure that Guinea . . . will be contributing with her quota to the wellbeing of the metropole."[17]

Cabral's landmark study of the agricultural profile of Portuguese Guinea was published in 1956, two years after its completion, in the *Boletim cultural da Guiné Portuguesa*, the journal of the Portuguese Guinea Studies Center, the executive commission of which he was a member. Besides his key involvement in conducting the census, Cabral also published ten articles on agronomy and related themes in the *Boletim* and the *Ecos da Guiné*. Altogether, within a decade of his first publication on rainfall in Cabo Verde in 1949, his published writings on agronomy and agriculture totaled about sixty works. Meanwhile, five months after completing the agricultural census, Cabral participated in an international conference on the peanut crop in Bambey, Senegal, where he presented two papers on the cultivation of this important West African export commodity.

The 1953 agricultural profile of Portuguese Guinea delineated by Cabral showed that the production of food crops, principally rice, occupied 76 percent of land use, while export crops, mainly peanuts, covered 23 percent of the total of 410,801 hectares, or 12 percent of the surface area of the colony. The coastal Balantas and Manjacos were responsible for 73 percent of the annual production of 100,000 tons of rice, while the Fulas and Mandinkas of the interior accounted for 66 percent of the annual cultivation of 64,000 tons of peanuts. Significantly, Cabral stressed the importance of rice cultivation for the food security and wellbeing of the indigenous population, as opposed to production of peanuts, which caused soil degradation and undermined traditional farming.

Cabral faced formidable challenges to implementing his hidden political agenda in a country where he was generally seen as yet another Cabo Verdean enabler of Portugal's harsh colonial rule. In the first place, the colonial context was such that the colonized "heathens" were naturally suspicious of colonial officials. They had learnt that questions about land use, livelihoods, and livestock could have serious implications—such as the obligation to pay taxes and submit to forced labor. Since the majority of the *chefes de posto*, the middle-level colonial officials in closest contact with the colonized, were Cabo Verdeans, Cabral faced the challenge of overcoming the almost automatic distrust the "uncivilized natives" had of the people they viewed as the colonizers. As the frontline operators of the native-rule system, these officials were often local tyrants. Their almost absolute powers meant direct and regular interference with the daily lives of the subjugated through the use of pliable *regulos* (local chiefs) and zealous *cipaios* (native administrative policemen). Defiance invariably met with summary corporal punishment through whippings and beatings. The *palmatoria*, a wooden paddle with holes to suck in flesh and make the beating more damaging, and the *chicote*, the hippo-hide whip, were favorite tools of correction.

Cabral witnessed several instances of colonial abuse while conducting the agricultural census. For example, in May 1953, while on the Bijagós island of Orango Grande, he found himself forced to stop the beating of an uncooperative elderly woman. Expressing his abhorrence of violence, he later manifested solidarity with the defiant victims who, "wounded in their human dignity, deprived of any legal personality," seized every opportunity "to manifest their non-acceptance of, aversion for and resistance to the Portuguese presence in Guinea."[18] Three months earlier, Cabral had been filled with indignation at the colonial bent for violence that resulted in the Batepá Massacre (3 February 1953) on the island of São Tomé, when hundreds of indigenous inhabitants were killed for refusing to be recruited as cacao plantation contract workers.

While the social dimension of agricultural production in Portuguese Guinea greatly concerned Cabral, the raising of political consciousness and mobilization for emancipatory politics was in fact his major preoccupation. Agronomy fulfilled a professional need, but politics was in fact the stronger passion. As he later pointed out, his return to his *terra natal* was "not by chance"; rather, "everything had been calculated." Acceptance of a position as second-class agronomist was a choice based on a commitment "to follow a calculation, the idea of doing something, to make a contribution to arousing the people for struggle against the Portuguese."[19]

In an attempt to safely navigate the dangerous colonial terrain and initiate the process of "conscientization," Cabral tried to form a sports and recreation club exclusively for the "sons of Guinea," irrespective of their legal status as "civilized" or "uncivilized." As a soccer enthusiast, he knew the game's capacity to bolster self-confidence, nurture collaboration, and foster camaraderie, which he considered critical factors of political mobilization. The PIDE was quick to perceive the fundamental purpose of Cabral's proposed club: "To launch the bases of an organization of natives, binding them in the same faith and the same destinies."[20] Not surprisingly, when the statutes of the club were submitted for approval, the colonial authorities promptly rejected them.

Although Cabral failed to create a soccer club, he would later use the game as a teaching aid to illustrate the importance of "unity and struggle." Using as illustration a soccer team that would comprise significant diversity—"different temperaments, often different education, some cannot read or write . . . different religion"—he underscored the critical cooperation and teamwork needed to "act together to score goals." Without unity of purpose, he insisted, there is no soccer team. The armed struggle was thus analogous to a soccer match between the colonizer and the colonized, and

PAIGC as the "national team" had to win by solid unity and relentless struggle.[21]

Cabral hastily left Portuguese Guinea with his wife and two-year-old daughter on 18 March 1955, in a medical evacuation for a serious bout of malaria. Shortly before his illness, he had a meeting with the discontented Governor Diogo Mello e Alvim, who warned him to "be careful" and "quit subversive activities, because this can cause you many setbacks." The governor knew about the "group with a cultural facade" he had formed, besides seeking "to get mixed up in politics" while conducting agricultural surveys in the rural areas. Cabral was ominously warned to "be careful."[22]

While in Lisbon, Cabral was prescribed a two-month period of convalescence that was later extended for another two months. His expected return to Bissau three days after the expiration of his recovery period did not happen because his contract with the Overseas Ministry was ended by "mutual consent" in July but this only became official on 7 September 1955.[23] Thus, Cabral was never expelled or temporarily exiled from Portuguese Guinea, although the prospects for his return in whatever capacity were not good. A report on his activities during the three years he spent there had been sent to the PIDE in Lisbon, highlighting his anticolonial posture, his "exaltation of the priority of the rights of the natives" and the belief that he "intended and succeeded, together with other natives, in the foundation

of the Sports and Recreation Association of Bissau."[24]
He was now under closer surveillance.

Now based in Lisbon, Cabral busied himself for
the next five years with consultancy work in Portugal
and Angola. A close collaborator of Cabral in numerous field studies in Angola was his former ISA professor
Ário Lobo de Azevedo, who commended him for his
"solid intelligence" and for having been "an applied student, conscientious and honest."[25]

Cabral's first consultancy work in Angola was for
the Sociedade Agrícola do Cassequel, a six-month as-
signment to map the soils of the Catumbelo valley. A
day after his arrival in the capital Luanda, on 29 August
1955, he wrote a letter to his wife scathingly criticizing
the Portuguese colonial presence. Astonished by "the
most miserable things that one can imagine regarding the colonial environment," Cabral described a city
where the "poor natives" lived "deplorably" and "the taxi
drivers, the servants in the hotels, restaurants, and cafes,
etc." were "all Europeans," with very few salaried jobs left
for the Africans. He denounced the "misery of all kinds"
and "the dirtiest of racism," which he found "nauseat-
ing." But he remained sanguine about the prospects for
transformative changes, "for the redemption on Earth
of these beings who vegetate here."[26]

Between 1955 and 1959, Cabral conducted numerous field studies in Angola for other entities including
the Companhia de Açúcar de Angola and the Companhia Angolana de Agricultura. While the consultancy

work enriched his professional life, his face-to-face encounter with the abject conditions of the majority of Angolans bolstered his commitment to anticolonial struggle.

In contact with local Angolan nationalists, including Viriato da Cruz, Cabral collaborated in the clandestine founding in Luanda of the Party of the Unified Struggle of the Africans of Angola (PLUAA) in November 1956. The manifesto of the PLUAA declared that "Portuguese colonialism will not fall without struggle" and exhorted Angolan nationalists to form a united front of "all the anti-imperialist forces of Angola, without regard to political colors, the social situation of individuals, religious beliefs, and philosophical tendencies of individuals," behind "the broadest popular movement for the liberation of Angola."[27] This became the origin of the Popular Movement for the Liberation of Angola (MPLA) that emerged as an operational liberation movement in 1960.

Cabral was also in contact with the Guinean and Cabo Verdean nationalists he left in Portuguese Guinea, especially his brother Luís and Aristides Pereira. The official narrative of the PAIGC maintains that, while Cabral was visiting his mother and siblings in Bissau, he cofounded its predecessor, the PAI, together with Aristides Pereira, Fernando Fortes, Rafael Barbosa, Elisée Turpin, and his brother Luís, on 19 September 1956. The Bissau-Guinean historian Julião Soares Sousa, among others, contests the presence of Cabral in Bissau in 1956, and his participation in the creation of the PAI, for lack of corroborating evidence.[28] On the other hand, Mário de Andrade has noted that, since the existence of the PAI was a closely guarded secret, "one would find no *written* trace of the date of its appearance inside or outside the frontiers of Guiné and Cape Verde" (emphasis in original).[29] Since the creation of an anticolonial movement in a colony ruled by a repressive colonial regime can only be done with the strictest secrecy, it is not implausible that Cabral could have been in Portuguese Guinea and clandestinely moved around to evade the surveillance of the PIDE. With the PAI apparently founded exactly a week after Cabral's thirty-second birthday, it is highly probable that he was in Bissau not least to visit and celebrate his birthday with his mother and siblings. Although on the watch list of the PIDE, he was nevertheless free to travel and had the financial means to do so.

Cabral was adept in eluding arrest by the tightening dragnet of the PIDE. Since his student days in Lisbon, he had always been hyperalert and sagacious compared to his closest comrades who ended up in jail. With the menacing words of Governor Mello e Alvin still fresh in his mind, Cabral had to be extremely cautious. Already in 1954, there were five PIDE agents in Bissau building a network of local informants. But even before the arrival of the notorious secret police, the inhabitants of the territory were under the watchful eyes of the brutal Public Security Police (PSP) and the hated *cipaios*. Recalling this period, Aristides Pereira underscored the climate of suspicion and mistrust that hung over Bissau when he was part of a small group of nationalists, some of whom he never met: "I knew that there were more people but never saw them. For example, I knew of Rafael Barbosa, but we never saw each other. It was a special situation, there was a sense of much mistrust in the air that obliged us to be always suspicious."[30]

According to Pereira, it was in the nondescript house he shared with fellow Cabo Verdean Fernando Fortes at 9C Rua Guerra Junqueira, situated on an unpaved street in the center of Bissau, where, on the evening of 19 September 1956, Amílcar and his brother Luís, together with the Guinean nationalists Rafael Barbosa and Júlio Almeida, met with Pereira and Fortes and founded the PAI. For security reasons, no minutes of the meeting were taken. Cabral, the architect of the political project, spoke of the creation of the secret movement as based on the historical and cultural links between Portuguese Guinea and Cabo Verde and "the fact that we continue to be subjected to domination by the same colonial power." As committed nationalists, its members should be "capable of uniting our two peoples." Otherwise, Cabral insisted, "the colonialists would eventually take Guineans to fight against the Cabo Verdean in Cabo Verde," and, likewise, use the islanders to fight the people of his *terra natal*. He emphasized the need for a united front of all the peoples of the Portuguese African colonies. While liberation movements should be created, Cabral entreated, "we must also have a party, with its minimum program and its maximum program." He then moved that "we create an African party of independence and union of the peoples of Guiné and Cabo Verde, whose motto will be unity and struggle."[31]

Cabral was named the PAI's first secretary-general and Barbosa its first president. In 1960, the Partido Africano da Independência (African Independence Party) would become the Partido Africano da Independência da Guiné e Cabo Verde (African Party for the Independence of Guinea and Cabo Verde), in a calculated move to advertise its inherent binationalism.

Binationalism in Action

Passive Resistance and
War Preparations, 1956–63

The founding of the PAI coincided with the opening session of the First International Conference of Negro Writers and Artists (19–22 September 1956), cosponsored by the journal *Présence africaine* and held at the University of Paris–Sorbonne, with participants from the "Negro World" who included the Senegalese Alioune Diop, Léopold Sédar Senghor, and Cheikh Anta Diop, the Martinicans Aimé Césaire and Frantz Fanon, the Haitians Jacques Stephen Alexis and Jean Price-Mars, and the Americans William Fontaine and Richard Wright (W. E. B. Du Bois and Paul Robeson could not attend because they were not issued passports). The deliberations at the four-day landmark event denounced colonialism and urged the formulation of a strategy "to make our culture into a force of liberation and solidarity."[1] Declared by Diop as the "Bandung culturel" ("cultural Bandung," a reference to the previous year's conference of African and Asian states held in Bandung, Indonesia), it was followed three years later by the Second International Conference of Negro Writers and Artists in Rome, which declared that "political independence and economic freedom are the indispensable prerequisites of fecund cultural development . . . in the countries of black Africa in particular."[2] Although Cabral did not attend these two important gatherings, he was nevertheless kept abreast of their developments and outcomes by the point person of the emergent anticolonial front, Mário de Andrade, who had escaped the wide net of the PIDE in 1954 and enrolled as a social science student at the University of Paris–Sorbonne.

In April 1955, a month after Cabral was medically evacuated from Bissau, the Bandung Conference had commenced its weeklong deliberations—yet another favorable external factor in the struggle for decolonization, with its pledges of support to anticolonial forces in the two continents. Four months earlier, the radical British journalist and historian Basil Davidson had published his soon to be influential book, *The African Awakening*, which presented a scathing criticism of Portuguese colonial practices. Cabral would meet Davidson in London five years later and the two would develop an enduring friendship during which the Englishman would travel with the PAIGC guerrillas and report on their war against the Portuguese.

Cabral went to Paris in November 1957 to collaborate with de Andrade, dos Santos, da Cruz, and others in the creation of the National Liberation Movement of the Portuguese Colonies (MLNCP). Significantly, this occurred after the Fifth Congress of the Portuguese Communist Party (PCP) two months earlier, which passed a resolution declaring "unconditional acknowledgement of the right of the peoples of the colonies of Africa dominated by Portugal to immediate and complete independence."[3] Thereafter, "true support" could only be expected from the Portuguese communists, since the rest of "the so-called Portuguese Opposition" was "as colonialist as fascist Salazar."[4] The MLNCP was preceded by the Lisbon-based and PCP-influenced Democratic Movement of the Portuguese Colonies (MDCP), formed mainly by Angolan students led by Neto, de Andrade, and Lúcio Lara in 1954, when Cabral was still in Portuguese Guinea. In early 1958, these two movements merged to form the Anticolonialist Movement (MAC), which had sections in three European cities: Lisbon, headed by Cabral and Neto; Paris, overseen by de Andrade and dos Santos; and Frankfurt, coordinated by Lara and da Cruz. For the next two years, these African nationalists in Western Europe would be busy carrying out the MAC mission of denouncing Portuguese colonialism in Africa.

The leadership of the MAC, through the key position of de Andrade as the secretary of the influential Alioune Diop, had access to the prominent figures of the "Negro World"—in particular, the Negritude founders Senghor and Césaire, the stalwart Pan-Africanists Kwame Nkrumah and Ahmed Sékou Touré, and the revolutionary theorist and practitioner Frantz Fanon. It was Fanon who, in the name of the recently established Provisional Government of the Algerian Republic—the government-in-exile of the Algerian National Liberation Front (FLN) headed by Ahmed Ben Bella—offered to have eleven MPLA militants trained by FLN fighters. Cabral was entrusted with conveying the Algerian offer to the Angolan nationalists in Luanda, but upon his arrival there in September 1959 the leaders he had to contact had already been arrested by the PIDE.

Cabral participated in the All-African People's Conference, in Accra, in December 1958, and together with the other MAC delegates made presentations on the nature of Portuguese colonialism. He appealed for material support of "our brothers in the interior facing the greatest obstacles," who needed "to feel supported." With the favorable outcome of the landmark conference whose host, Kwame Nkrumah, promised political and diplomatic support, Cabral concluded that "in Accra, things went very well."[5] And after pledging "some money, although little," as his personal contribution to the operating expenses of the MAC, Cabral cautioned his comrades to remain alert in the face of the tightening vigilance of the PIDE, confiding, "I don't know up to what point I am being watched."[6] A year later, following the massacre of striking dockworkers at the port of Pindjiguiti in Bissau, his name was high up in the most-wanted list of the PIDE.

The brutal shootings on 3 August 1959 of the Pindjiguiti stevedores and merchant sailors who refused to return to work without a satisfactory resolution of their demands for better salaries and working conditions marked yet another crucial turning point in the life of Cabral. In Bissau, a month after the bloody Pindjiguiti event he called "the most heinous crime," Cabral reported to his MAC comrades in Europe that "the slaughter" carried out by the colonial forces left "24 dead and 35 wounded, some gravely."[7] Later, a PAIGC narrative would indicate "50 dead and over 100 wounded,"[8] while the colonial authorities maintained that it was "nine dead and 14 wounded."[9] Yet, in spite of the discrepancy, the Pindjiguiti Massacre became as decisively shattering for the Guinean nationalists as the Boston Massacre of 1770, with five dead and six wounded, was for the American patriots. Both these incidents were quickly used as effective political propaganda to ignite anticolonial fervor. Amílcar Cabral secretly met with the PAI leadership on 19 September 1959 and together they vowed to take revenge for the massacre: "We swore in silence to avenge our martyrs, the first sacrifices for the liberation of our country."[10]

The Pindjiguiti Massacre led to the jettisoning of the hitherto nonviolent strategy of the PAI. It seemed obvious that the Portuguese colonizers were not only uninterested in a dialogue on decolonization, but manifestly hostile to the very idea of their departure from Africa. Cabral and the PAI leadership thus had no problem reaching the conclusion that liberation from Portuguese colonial domination could only be achieved "through struggle by all means possible, including war."[11] Cabral considered the most important lesson of the massacre to be the imperative to "mobilize and organize the rural masses," rather than the urban-based salaried workers, for the inevitable armed liberation struggle.[12]

Vowing to struggle relentlessly "until unconditional victory against our oppressors,"[13] Cabral left for Lisbon to prepare for his definite relocation, together with his family, to Conakry, where, ten months before the Pindjiguiti Massacre, Sékou Touré had presided over the celebrations of Guinea's achievement of independence. Before the trip to Portugal, Cabral made a brief stop in Conakry to update himself on the diplomatic relations being established between the government of President Sékou Touré and the MAC, whose local representative was the São Toméan medical doctor Hugo de Menezes. The Conakry-Guinean authorities had been very accommodating and the MAC was even officially represented at the Democratic Party of Guinea's fifth congress, during which the ruling party solidified its dominance over the new nation's political landscape. Excited by the enabling conditions being created by the sanctuary nation, Cabral informed his comrades in Europe that "more than ever, I am sure of the need and advantages of our presence here, among our brothers."[14]

Cabral left Lisbon in early January 1960 to dedicate himself entirely to the cause of national liberation. He headed for Paris, where his wife and daughter joined him; however, after a few days together an uneasy Cabral persuaded Maria Helena to return with Mariva to Lisbon, where he believed they would be safer, while he would be freer to pursue his political agenda. Although Cabral had cleverly managed to elude arrest and detention, he was nevertheless acutely aware of being under active watch in Portugal, which meant that he was not quite safe in France or any Western European nation, especially the NATO member countries, given the close collaboration between their security and intelligence apparatuses. After the return of his family to Portugal, Cabral embarked for Tunisia to attend the Second All-African People's Conference (25–30 January 1960).

Starting on the day Congolese nationalist leader Patrice Lumumba, released from a six-month prison sentence less than twenty-four hours earlier, was flown to Brussels to participate in the Belgo-Congolese Round Table Conference that would concede independence to his country within six months, the Tunis conference marked the beginning of Cabral's full-time engagement as a revolutionary nationalist and Pan-Africanist. Considering the Pan-African gathering as an opportunity "to open African doors" that would facilitate the MAC's mission of "the internationalization of our political situation," Cabral and Mário de Andrade prepared a memorandum for the MAC delegates that framed the contents of their presentations. The conference coincided with the visit to Tunisia of UN Secretary-General Dag Hammarskjöld, who a month earlier had been sent a telegram by the MAC leadership requesting him to inform the UN General Assembly's Special Political and Decolonization Committee (Fourth Committee) of the "systematic atrocities and nefarious murders against the African people of Guinea and Angola." Among the eight priorities for the MAC outlined were the needs (a) to act as "a single front, representative of our peoples"; (b) to inform the conference of the reality of Portuguese colonialism and Portugal's "negative attitude toward the liberation of our people and toward the responsibilities demanded of her by the United Nations Charter"; and (c) to demonstrate that the struggle against Portuguese colonialism "is today the most important for the liquidation of colonialism in Africa." Furthermore, Cabral exhorted his comrades to insist that "Pan-Africanism and African solidarity make no sense" if the independent African nations "do not engage decisively and positively in this struggle."[15]

Significantly, for the first time, an international conference held in Africa adopted a resolution condemning Portugal's colonial policies and practices, reaffirming the rights of the colonized Africans to national independence, and urging the independent governments of Africa to provide "unconditional support." The resolution also demanded the immediate release of all political prisoners in all the five colonies.

At the end of the Tunis conference, Cabral and his comrades founded the African Revolutionary Front for the National Independence of the Portuguese Colonies (FRAIN), described as "an alliance of political parties and mass organizations" struggling for independence from Portugal. The umbrella organization emphatically stated its mission as "the immediate conquest of the national independence of the African countries under Portuguese colonial domination and the total liquidation of Portuguese colonialism in Africa." Unlike the MAC it succeeded, there was clarity on how such an objective was to be achieved: nonviolence and civil disobedience, but with "resort to reprisals against violence."[16] The founding political parties were the PAI and the MPLA, notwithstanding the presence at the conference of the Union of the Peoples of Angola (UPA), represented by its founder and leader, Holden Roberto. The UPA's nonmembership in the FRAIN at its creation was largely due to the negative perception and mistrust that the radical nationalists had of its leader, who Cabral scathingly denounced as "a traitor and a bandit" for having been given "everything" in Accra by Kwame Nkrumah's government, including a house and an office, and for the fact that, in Cabral's words, "he never did anything."[17] Nevertheless, following a meeting with Cabral and his comrades, who were more concerned with being seen as a united front against Portuguese colonialism, Roberto jointly signed the Declaration of Commitment that the FRAIN founders drafted. The declaration tasked the FRAIN with coordinating "the revolutionary action of patriotic Africans" and exhorted the signatory movements to jointly struggle against Portuguese colonialism, irrespective of ideological differences.

The member movements committed to refrain from taking unilateral actions that could significantly compromise "our common struggle against our common enemy, Portuguese colonialism."

Cabral left Tunis for London, and his trip to the capital of the world's largest colonial power was the beginning of a sustained diplomatic offensive to garner international support. Notwithstanding its status as an imperialist power, Great Britain had a long tradition of liberalism that constitutionally enshrined fundamental freedoms which, since the nineteenth century, had attracted exiles of various ideological persuasions from all corners of the world. For more than a decade since the late 1940s, London was abuzz with anticolonial activities, among many other political agitations. With the state visit of Portuguese president Francisco Craveiro Lopes in October 1955, reciprocated by Queen Elizabeth two years later, Cabral was intent on exposing the nature of Portugal's colonial rule in Africa.

Cabral's task was made easier by the contacts established with the Committee of African Organizations run by anticolonial African activists and supported by civil society and political organizations including the Movement for Colonial Freedom, Christian Action, and the Communist Party of Great Britain, besides individual members of the Labor Party, the Liberal Party, and the labor unions. Basil Davidson was among the numerous Britons who formed the critical mass of progressives that actively supported the anti-imperialist and anticolonial struggles, especially in Africa. Thus, when Cabral arrived in London, the prevailing environment was sufficiently enabling for him to publish, under the pseudonym of Abel Djassi, a pamphlet titled *The Facts about Portugal's African Colonies*, with an introduction by Davidson.

Prefaced by the denunciation that there were eleven million Africans under an oppressive fascist colonial system that made them "live on a sub-human standard—little or no better than serfs in their own country," Cabral stated unequivocally the demands of his fellow African nationalists.[18]

> We, the Africans of the Portuguese colonies . . .
> want Portugal to respect and rigidly adhere to the
> obligations set out in the UN Charter. We demand
> that Portugal should follow the example of Britain,
> France, and Belgium in recognizing the right of the
> peoples she dominates to self-determination and
> independence.

Aiming at sensitizing the British government and public to put pressure on the Lisbon regime, however unlikely that might have been, Cabral further pointed out that the nationalist movements of the Portuguese colonies wanted "to re-establish the human dignity of Africans, their freedom, and the right to determine their own future," objectives to be achieved through "peaceful means." However, he and his fellow nationalist leaders were under no illusion, since they were sure that "Portugal intends to use violence to defend her interests," against which they would be ready "to answer with violence." The psychological preparedness of Cabral and his fellow nationalist leaders for armed liberation struggle was thus made explicit, and he would soon head to the Republic of Guinea to prepare for the seemingly inevitable war.

While in Paris en route to Conakry, Cabral wrote to his wife urging her to hasten her definitive departure from Portugal, together with their daughter, to France, where they would wait for their imminent voyage to Conakry. She would improve her French in Paris in preparation for life in Francophone Guinea-Conakry. With the family travel arrangements made, he left for Dakar on 5 May 1960, arriving there on the same day as his brother Luís, who had escaped imminent arrest in Bissau by the PIDE. Married two years earlier to Lucette Andrade, a Senegalese of Cabo Verdean parents, Luís would get a job as a bookkeeper for the Shell Oil Company. He would also become the point person for the PAI in the capital of the newly independent Senegal.

Cabral arrived in Conakry in mid-May to face enormous challenges that would test his personal integrity, intellectual capacity, and leadership qualities. Besides the immediate diplomatic, organizational, and logistical problems he had to deal with in the process of building a solid foundation for the headquarters of the PAI and a base for launching the armed struggle, he quickly found himself embroiled in the "Battle of Conakry."

This was a sustained four-year campaign (1960–63) waged by his political foes from the rival nationalist organizations that were forced to abandon Bissau following the Pindjiguiti Massacre of 3 August 1959. The activists of the short-lived Movement for the National Independence of Portuguese Guinea (MING), founded clandestinely in Bissau in the mid-1950s by Cabral and others, variously went on to create the PAI, the Liberation Movement of Guinea (MLG), and the Liberation Movement of Guinea and Cabo Verde (MLGCV). Factionalism, fueled by personality clashes, ideological differences, and narrow nationalism, was rife within these and other emergent groups. The PAI, predominantly led by nationalists of Cabo Verdean descent, were opportunistically targeted because of the role of the "Portuguese Cabo Verdeans" in the colonial domination of Portuguese Guinea. Cabral, with legitimate birthright claims in both Portuguese Guinea and Cabo Verde, was constantly suspected by the more petty patriots of both countries. The sometimes vicious campaigns of delegitimization questioned not his credentials and capacity but his racial identity.

Parallel to the hostility toward "the Cabo Verdeans" in Conakry was the "Battle of Dakar," wherein the PAIGC's rival organizations launched an equally intense campaign of discrediting and delegitimization. Among the most vocal opponents of Cabral and his party was the Liberation Movement of Guinea–Dakar (MLG-Dakar), founded in Dakar in 1960 by François Kankoila Mendy, which later affiliated with the Front for Struggle for the National Independence of Guinea (FLING), also created in Dakar (3 August 1962). The FLING was an umbrella organization of some seven Bissau-Guinean nationalist groups that included the MLG-Dakar, the Union of the Populations of So-Called Portuguese Guinea (UPGP) headed by Henry Labéry, and the Union of the Natives of Portuguese Guinea (UNGP) led by Benjamin Pinto Bull. Under the leadership of Labéry, the FLING coalition became the most formidable rival of the PAIGC. However, while the MLG-Dakar was the only militarily active member of the FLING, launching attacks against Portuguese posts in the northern border towns of Susana, Varela, São Domingos, and Bigene in 1961 and 1962 with ineffectual outcomes, the anti-PAIGC coalition would be notable for its advocacy of a nonviolent negotiated path to independence. One of its leaders, Benjamin Pinto Bull, would be delegated in July 1963 to meet with Salazar, who refused to discuss the independence of any "overseas province."

Meanwhile, Cabral responded to the concerted campaigns of delegitimization by rising above the personal attacks and striving to undermine the collaborationist activities of his rivals through the formation of anticolonial coalitions like the United Liberation Front (FUL), created in Dakar in July 1961 and comprising several nationalist organizations, including Mendy's MLG-Dakar. The FUL collapsed a year later due to factionalist conflicts and hostility toward Cabo Verdeans. Ironically, the efforts to discredit Cabral's Bissau-Guinean origins were rendered ridiculous by the fact that Mendy and Labéry, his staunchest adversaries, were both born in Senegal, each with one parent who was not of Bissau-Guinean origins. Importantly, within the PAIGC, the anti–Cabo Verdean sentiment was also present and vulnerable to fatal exploitation.

With the collapse of the FUL in 1962, Cabral concentrated his energy on preparations to launch an effective long-term strategy of armed struggle at the political, diplomatic, and military levels. The Angolan uprisings in February 1961 initiated the war against the Portuguese colonial empire in Africa. The Estado Novo regime intuitively viewed the Angolan insurrection as an insult to the sovereignty of the nation, much-lauded as "pluricontinental" and "pluriracial." The MLG-Dakar attacks in northern Portuguese Guinea exacerbated the perceived affront. These "offenses" would turn into humiliations when recently independent Dahomey (present-day Benin) seized the former Portuguese slave-trading port of São João Baptista de Ajudá in August 1961. Four months later, the forceful annexation of the Portuguese enclaves of Goa, Damão, and Diu by India would augment Lisbon's embarrassment. The abrupt ending of over 450 years of Portugal's sovereignty in the territories referred to as the Estado da India (State of India) exploded the myth of a timeless and inviolable empire.

The PAIGC's mobilization campaigns started in earnest following the training of the mobilizers at

Cabral's house in the Minière neighborhood of Conakry soon after his installation in the Guinean capital, where his wife and daughter had joined him shortly after his arrival. The Cabrals stayed together only briefly. Expecting their second child, Maria Helena, who had been employed as a teacher in a local high school, moved with Iva to Rabat, Morocco, for better medical attention during the birth of Ana Luísa, born in 1962. The prolonged separation ended in divorce in 1966. At the end of that year, Cabral married Ana Maria Voss de Sá, a native of Canchungo, Portuguese Guinea, who was a student activist and an affiliate of the House of Students of the Empire (CEI) and the Center for African Studies (CEA) in Lisbon, where they became acquainted. A militant of the PAIGC, Ana Maria underwent university training in Czechoslovakia. In 1969, the couple had a daughter, N'Dira Abel.

Initially, the Cabrals' house in Conakry was transformed into a makeshift school, with Amílcar largely responsible for program content and the few instructors including his wife Maria Helena, his brother Luís, sister-in-law Lucette, and close associate Aristides Pereira. The majority of the students, mostly poor, illiterate young men and women from the countryside, went through an intense literacy program, while the literate urban recruits were trained in persuasive techniques informed by lectures on geography, nationalist history and politics, the principles of the PAIGC, and the aims and objectives of the upcoming armed struggle.

Later, Cabral would secure financial support to acquire a Lar dos Combatentes (Home of the Fighters) situated in the Bonfi neighborhood of Conakry, where the party's young mobilizers were trained and temporarily lodged. This was followed by the establishment of an Escola Piloto (Pilot School), a boarding school opened in 1965 to provide for the education of the children of militants and combatants. The first director of the school was Maria da Luz "Lilica" Boal, a Cabo Verdean from the island of Santiago who, as a politically active history and philosophy student in Lisbon, abandoned her studies in 1961 and left with her Angolan husband, a medical doctor, to join the PAIGC in Conakry. Among the first group of students enrolled in the Pilot School was Florentino "Flora" Gomes, who went on to become a world-renowned filmmaker.

Before his arrest on 13 March 1962, Rafael Barbosa, the president of the PAIGC who stayed in Bissau operating under the pseudonym of Zain Lopes, sent to Conakry some five hundred young city dwellers, most of them belonging to the déclassé category identified by Cabral as recently arrived rural-urban migrants with connections to "petty bourgeois" and wage earners. The usefulness of this group for the mobilization campaigns was its unbroken connection with the rural world. Of the other city dwellers without such close connection with the countryside, who often had at least primary school education, some would go on to hold key positions in the leadership of the PAIGC, including Francisco

"Tchico Te" Mendes, João Bernardo Vieira, Domingos Ramos, Carmen Pereira, and Francisca Pereira. About one thousand party militants were trained at the political school in Conakry.

The political mobilization campaigns launched by Cabral from Conakry were well planned. Profiting from the harsh lived experiences of the rural population, the trained mobilizers initially descended on the southern and northern regions of Portuguese Guinea, covering village by village, asking questions aimed at heightening consciousness, provoking outrage, and invoking rebelliousness. The rehearsed dialogue avoided, as Cabral insisted, giving the peasants the impression that the mobilizers were "strangers who had come to teach them lessons." Instead, they had to behave like they were there to learn. Listening empathetically in order to gain the confidence of the villagers, the questions mobilizers posed were meant to allow the villagers themselves to reach the conclusion "that there is exploitation." Using "a direct language that all can understand," the mobilizers asked questions including the following:

> What is the situation? Did you pay taxes? Did your
> father pay taxes? What have you seen from those taxes?
> How much do you get for your groundnuts? . . . How
> much sweat has it cost your family? Which of you
> have been imprisoned? You are going to work on road
> construction: who gives you the tools? You bring the
> tools. Who provides your meals? You provide your

meals? But who walks on the road? Who has a car? And your daughter who was raped?—are you happy about that?[19]

Cabral's political mobilization strategy was largely successful, in spite of the life-threatening dangers that its deployment entailed. The challenges included the noncooperation of some villagers, especially those from the more stratified Fula, Mandinka, and Manjaco societies, where most of the traditional chiefs collaborated with the Portuguese and their loyal followers became informers, resulting in the arrest, torture, and killing of PAIGC mobilizers. On the other hand, the brutal repressions by the colonial authorities obliged some villagers to shun the mobilizers for security reasons: "You come here telling us very beautiful things, but you are not capable of defending us."[20] Nevertheless, the mobilization drive had to run its course. Cabral knew that its success ultimately rested on the internalization by his mobilizers of the imperative to "never confuse what they have in their heads with reality," that the point of departure must always be "from the reality of our land—to be realists." Sophisticated rhetoric about "colonial exploitation" and exhortatory slogans like "land to the landless," while effective in the settler colonies of Angola and Mozambique, had little resonance in Portuguese Guinea. Cabral knew that winning the hearts and minds of an oppressed people and maintaining their active support for armed struggle must be contingent on the recognition and ready acceptance of their fundamental expectations. Thus, he exhorted both mobilizers and combatants:

> Always remember that the people are not fighting for ideas, nor for what is in men's minds. The people fight and accept the sacrifices demanded by the struggle in order to gain material advantages, to live better and in peace, to benefit from progress, and for the better future of their children. National liberation, the struggle against colonialism, the construction of peace, progress and independence are hollow words devoid of any significance unless they can be translated into a real improvement of living conditions.[21]

The war preparations conducted by Cabral from Conakry also entailed military training abroad for the liberation fighters, particularly in the communist countries of the People's Republic of China (PRC), the USSR, and Cuba. The first batch of ten young fighters departed for the PRC in February 1961 to train at the Nanjing Military Academy. They included João Bernardo "Nino" Vieira, Osvaldo Vieira, Domingos Ramos, Francisco "Tchico Te" Mendes, Constantino Teixeira, and Vitorino da Costa. They would return to conduct the armed struggle and become celebrated national heroes. In the context of the intense Sino-Soviet rivalry, this significant achievement was testimony to Cabral's great diplomatic skill and strength of character. He also succeeded in obtaining military assistance from African countries including Ghana, Morocco, and Algeria—the first to supply guns and ammunition to the PAIGC.

The Republic of Guinea, the host country, provided not only a safe haven for Cabral and his comrades to train the party's cadres, mobilizers, and school-age children, but also the use of its military training facilities for its fighters, besides rendering vital political and diplomatic support. Conakry was the propitious place where Cabral was able to forge enduring relations with the Chinese, Soviets, and Cubans, among others, relations that quickly translated into weapons, military training, and technical advisors. The remarkable achievements during this preparatory phase of the armed struggle were largely due to the goodwill and confidence bestowed on Cabral by President Sékou Touré. After skillfully outmaneuvering his most powerful rivals in Conakry, Cabral developed strong relations with Sékou Touré, facilitated by shared ideological outlooks.

Cabral was aware of the strategies and lessons of the successful post-1945 anti-imperialist and anticolonial wars, which he acknowledged "served us as a basis of general experience for our own struggle." But he was against "blindly applying the experience of others." In determining the tactics for the armed struggle, he noted, "we had to take into account the geographical, historical, economic, and social conditions of our own country."[22] Consequently, the war strategy had to be based on rural insurgency and sustained by a politically mobilized peasantry. It would be a "struggle of the people, by the people, for the people."[23] It would aim at not only destroying Portuguese military installations but also dislocating the colonial economy and, within the liberated areas, establishing structures and institutions for political governance, economic sustainability, and social cohesion. Importantly, it would also address the basic needs of the inhabitants to secure their sustained support. Furthermore, he made a distinction between "the struggle against imperialism" and "struggling for national liberation," associating the former with "national independence" and the latter, in which he and his comrades were engaged, with the imperative to go beyond "flag independence" and "struggle against neo-colonialism."[24]

In the context of the Cold War, Cabral envisaged "only two possible paths for an independent nation: to return to imperialist domination (neo-colonialism, capitalism, state capitalism), or to take the way of socialism."[25] The ideological orientation of the PAIGC, as presented by Cabral, was socialist in character, being very much influenced by the Marxist perspective. The program of the PAIGC devised largely by Cabral incorporated both short-term and long-tern goals, with the more urgent objectives including the achievement of political independence and those of a longer timeframe involving economic and social transformations and the unification of his two countries of birth and ancestry.

6

Conducting Armed Struggle

The Liberation of Portuguese Guinea, 1963–73

On 3 August 1961, the second anniversary of the Pindji-guiti Massacre, Cabral announced the PAIGC's passage "from the phase of political struggle to that of national insurrection, to direct action against the colonial forces." Taking stock of the high human cost of passive resis-tance, he declared that the struggle against the *Tugas* was no longer a question of whether it should be armed or unarmed, since the enemy "is always armed."[1] The critical question, he argued, was whether the Portuguese colonizers should continue to have the monopoly of the gun or "we get arms to shoot them also." Invoking the lesson of the 1959 massacre, he concluded, "This is the truth about the truth . . . as they showed us on the quay of Pindjiguiti."[2]

But Cabral was no bloodthirsty *terrorista* on a mis-sion of vengeful retribution, as he would be portrayed by Portuguese propaganda. He abhorred violence, which he only advocated as a last resort after several appeals to the Estado Novo for a peaceful path to independence.

He insisted on the use of "selective violence" that avoided "collateral damage" and exhorted his fighters to remember that the enemy was "Portuguese colonialism, represented by the colonial-fascist government of Portugal," and not the Portuguese people.[3] Therefore, the "direct action" should be "aimed only at the forces of repression (army, police and colonial agents)."[4]

Cabral continued with the political mobilization of the rural population for another six months. At the same time, he ordered a sabotage campaign involving the downing of telephone and telegraph lines and the destruction of bridges and roads in the southern region of Quinara. But he was still ready to negotiate independence with the Lisbon authorities. Addressing the UN Special Committee on Territories under Portuguese Administration meeting in Conakry held 5–7 June 1962, he declared that "the PAIGC still is and always has been desirous of reaching a peaceful solution of the conflict between them [the people of Guinea] and the government of Portugal."[5] Six months later, he traveled to New York and appeared before the UN Fourth Committee to reiterate his movement's readiness to negotiate: "On our part, we are ready for the contacts and for the negotiations, with or without intermediaries. We declare that we are still ready to negotiate in any place, including Portugal."[6]

But independence was not part of the lexicon of the Estado Novo. Portugal's geographic location and membership in NATO greatly favored the stubbornly intransigent position of the Salazar dictatorship. Situated in the westernmost part of Western Europe, the tiny Iberian country assumed a huge strategic importance in the defense architecture of the United States–led NATO. In particular, on her Atlantic islands of the Azores, the American base at Lajes not only monitored Soviet submarine movements in the Atlantic, but also served as a refueling stop for American military airlift operations to the Middle East and beyond. Washington's strategic priority became an important bargaining chip for the Lisbon authorities to obtain deadly weapons, including napalm and white phosphorous bombs, in order to sustain a brutal war in three African theaters for over a decade. "Everyone knows," Cabral derisively commented, "that Portugal does not make any aircraft, not even as toys for children."[7] Faced with a reality he and his comrades had to come to terms with, Cabral turned to the communist world to secure a steady supply of war material and supplies, particularly from the USSR, the PRC, Czechoslovakia, and Cuba. Thwarted in his numerous initiatives for a peaceful decolonization, Cabral and his comrades concentrated on "answering with violence the violence of the Portuguese colonialist forces and, by all the means possible, eliminating colonial domination from Guiné and Cabo Verde."[8]

Taking full advantage of the Cold War, Portugal dismissed the armed struggle as a communist orchestration emanating from "Moscow, Prague and Peking." A report by the International and State Defense Police

(PIDE) of 17 January 1963, submitted to the colonial authorities in Bissau six days before the launching of full-scale armed struggle by the PAIGC, warned about the danger of nationalist organizations that "receive orders and material support from the outside and are subordinated to international communism." It outlined the "subversive activities" of the PAIGC, whose militants were involved in "the rapid catechization of the masses" through widespread mobilization campaigns and engagements in "acts of terrorism."[9]

About a month before the PAIGC's transition to "direct action," the MLG-Dakar, led by François Kankoila Mendy, had staged a series of attacks on the small Portuguese garrison at São Domingos and the nearby resort towns of Varela and Susana. Governor António Augusto Peixoto Correia dismissed the insurgency as the actions of "armed bandits" who planned "to liberate Portuguese Guinea" but were opposed by the "indomitable will" of the colony's inhabitants, "who do not need this liberation."[10] Besides the five soldiers injured, numerous telephone lines cut, and several dwellings and government facilities set ablaze, the attacks also caused panic among the tiny white population in the colony, which hurriedly flocked to Bissau. The Portuguese were fearful of a rerun of the bloody uprising in northern Angola organized by Holden Roberto's Union of the Peoples of Angola (UPA) just four months earlier, which left a death toll of about a thousand Portuguese settlers indiscriminatingly massacred during the frenzied carnage that a despondent Cabral called "gratuitous violence." The swift and ferocious response of the colonial authorities and armed white civilians was equally gratuitous: "The greatest pleasure of certain whites is to kill blacks. When military trucks full of black prisoners arrive in Luanda, the white civilians shoot them down like dogs."[11]

With only 1,200 mostly native soldiers and no air force or navy in Portuguese Guinea in January 1961, the concerned Lisbon authorities quickly sent reinforcements that included a detachment of F-86 Sabre jet fighter planes provided to Portugal by the United States for NATO deployment in Europe. These were later complemented by American T-6 Texan light attack planes and West German–built Italian Fiat G-91 light attack fighter aircraft. By January 1963, the Portuguese military presence had swollen to 5,500 soldiers, including 311 marines and 354 air force personnel.

Although the attacks by the ill-trained MLG-Dakar fighters inaugurated the armed liberation struggle in Portuguese Guinea, they soon proved ineffective and unsustainable, being poorly armed and ineptly organized. Cabral promptly dismissed the attacks as hasty and adventurous. Nevertheless, Mendy's actions put some pressure on the PAIGC to operationalize its "direct action" program. However, Cabral's war preparations were not only inconclusive but still encountering serious challenges. Already in January 1962, the important task of securing war materiel had hit a serious snag when the Conakry-Guinean customs at the port of Conakry confiscated a concealed consignment of weapons and communications equipment sent from Morocco. Several PAIGC leaders were promptly arrested, including Aristides Pereira, Luís Cabral, Carlos Correia, and Armando Ramos. Cabral, who was attending the Third Afro-Asian Solidarity Conference in Tanzania, hastily returned to Conakry and skillfully negotiated the release of his comrades and the weapons. Most significantly, Cabral obtained official approval for the free importation of war supplies into the host country.

On 23 January 1963, under the banner of "unity and struggle," Cabral ordered his trained fighters to fire the first salvo of the war of national liberation. About twenty guerrillas led by Arafam Mané attacked the Portuguese garrison at Tite, in the Quinara region. The precursors to the "direct action" were the PIDE raids on the PAIGC office in Bissau and the homes of its activists, capturing, on 13 March 1962, the organization's president, Rafael Barbosa, and several of his comrades, together with important documents and a few weapons.[12] A curfew was expeditiously imposed on Bissau. Many of the captured nationalists, including Barbosa, would end up in the Tarrafal concentration camp in Santiago, Cabo Verde. Three months later, the colonial forces launched a brutal wave of repressions, which met with resistance. On 25 June, the PIDE reported that the Balantas in the southern border region of Tombali, "who have long been indoctrinated," had attacked the administrative town of Catió, destroyed a ferry in the town of Bedanda, and

Figure 1. Cabral the revolutionary theoretician: weaponizing theory and conducting war. Copyright, Bruna Polimeni (1971), Fondazione Lelio e Lisli Basso.

cut telephone lines. It was, the PIDE underscored, "the beginning of terrorist activities" in the south. Two days later, in the resistance to repression in the north of the country, a PIDE agent, Augusto Macias, was killed, and two of his colleagues and a police officer were injured. By the end of July, some two thousand nationalists were imprisoned by the PIDE, with two hundred and fifty of them sent to the Tarrafal concentration camp. But the resistance continued unabated.

The southern littoral region bordering northern Guinea-Conakry became the ideal part of the colony to intensify the armed struggle. As an experienced agronomist, Cabral knew very well its geography and topography, characterized by verdant vegetation with thick mangrove forests, abundant palm trees, and a network of waterways that include the rivers Geba, Grande, Corubal, Cacine, and their respective tributaries. The area was well suited for guerrilla insurgency.

As the repression escalated, Cabral ordered the intensification of political mobilization in the south, the impact of which was reflected in the PIDE report that the traditionally "chiefless" Balantas, predominantly rice farmers who had migrated to the area from the central and northern regions and formed the majority of its inhabitants, "continued to be catechized and advised to not work on the *bolhanas* [rice fields], with the justification that there will soon be war." The colonial forces descended heavily on the region and in the ensuing brutal repressions several PAIGC mobilizers were arrested, tortured, and some killed—among them, twenty-five-year-old Vitorino da Costa, recently returned from military training in the PRC. His decapitated head, like those of his comrades, was displayed on a spike to maximize the terrorization of the villagers.[13] But the "catechization of the masses"[14] continued unremittingly. The PIDE was now convinced that it was facing "a properly structured terrorist organization," trained in subversion and guerrilla warfare.[15]

The PAIGC dawn assault on the Tite garrison that formally opened the southern front was quickly followed by a series of actions, including attacks on military installations, ambushes, destruction of transport and communication infrastructure, and the capture, on 25 March 1963, of two commercial vessels at the port of

Cafine. The *Mirandela*, belonging to the Union Manufacturing Company (CUF) subsidiary Casa Gouveia, and the *Arouca*, owned by Casa Brandão, were respectively captained by company employees José Ocante da Silva and Joãozinho Lopes, survivors of the Pindjiguiti Massacre. The captured ships were taken to the nearby Guinea-Conakry port of Boké, with most of the crew and numerous dockworkers onboard—recruits for the armed liberation struggle. The vessels were later taken to Conakry and used to transport combatants and war material, thus becoming the first ships of the PAIGC navy.

The effectiveness of Cabral's military strategy in six months of full-scale war had, by the admission of the Portuguese, resulted in the liberation of 15 percent of the national territory, mostly in the south between the rivers Geba and Corubal. He had outwitted the colonial forces with a "centrifugal" war plan that caught them by surprise, which he explained thus: "We opted for a strategy we could call centrifugal: from the center to the periphery."[16] The Portuguese, on the other hand, expecting the MLG-Dakar tactic of cross-border attacks and withdrawal to safe havens in Senegal, had made the strategic miscalculation of stationing their troops in garrisons and fortified camps dotted along the borders. Cabral was now firmly establishing the credibility of his liberation movement not only internally but also internationally—especially among the member states of the recently created Organization of African Unity

(OAU), which aimed "to eradicate all forms of colonialism from Africa," in pursuance of which it established the African Liberation Committee to coordinate political and military support of independence movements in the continent.

The courage and tenacity of the PAIGC fighters was most severely tested when they confronted the enormous Portuguese firepower on the contested strategic onshore island of Como, in Tombali region, in December 1963. Cabral had appointed twenty-four-year-old João Bernardo "Nino" Vieira, a recent graduate of the Nanjing Military Academy, as the military commander of the southern front. Codenamed "Marga," Nino Vieira commanded the PAIGC force that captured Como, prompting the Portuguese to launch Operation Trident on 15 January 1964 to reoccupy the island. Besides its strategic significance for the protection of the commercial hub of Catió, Como had also allowed the Portuguese a location from which to monitor PAIGC activities in the south and the flow of weapons from across the border. Determined to prevent any "rebellion contagion," the colonial authorities organized a massive counteroffensive that was closely watched by some of the Portuguese top brass sent to Bissau from the military high command in Lisbon. Comprising three thousand soldiers, of which two thousand were elite troops hurriedly dispatched from Angola, supported by the Portuguese Air Force (FAP), the task force descended on Como to dislodge a guerrilla force of about three hundred fighters. The local population of mainly Balanta rice farmers supported the guerrillas. Recognizing the importance of victory at this early stage of the armed struggle, Cabral instructed his fighters to defend the island against the tremendous odds they faced.

After seventy-five days of fierce fighting during which the FAP pounded the island with over three hundred and fifty heavy bombs, targeting not only guerrillas and civilians but also rice fields, the reoccupation attempt was abandoned, with contested counts for Portuguese casualties: nine dead and forty-seven injured according to the Portuguese command; "losses of 650 men" according to the PAIGC. The toll for the freedom fighters was calculated at seventy-six dead and fifteen injured. An FAP T-6 Texan plane was downed and six more combat aircraft hit. The Lisbon authorities promptly fired Governor Vasco Martins Rodrigues and the military commander. The new governor, General Arnaldo Schulz—who assumed both of the vacated positions—vowed that "Guinea will never cease to be Portuguese."

The victory at Como, achieved without the cover of the rainy season (ideal for guerrilla warfare) and against an unfavorable balance of firepower, not only demonstrated the military capability of Cabral's liberation movement, but also bolstered its credibility and boosted the confidence of the freedom fighters. The PAIGC had demonstrated its capacity to conquer and defend territory. A jubilant Cabral would underscore that Como and the liberated areas in the south were "from now on *definitely liberated*" (emphasis in the original).[17]

Cabral's fighters were also attacking the Portuguese in the north of the country, where another front was opened in July 1962. The PAIGC forces were under the command of Osvaldo Vieira (cousin of Nino Vieira), with an operational base at Morés in the legendary region of Oio, famous for centuries as a center of resistance against Portuguese imperial ambitions, and only finally "pacified" in 1913.

With initiative and momentum on the side of Cabral's fighters, the colonial forces were fighting a defensive war in which they were steadily losing ground. Absolving himself of responsibility for the ineffectiveness of the colonial forces, the dismissed Portuguese military commander, Colonel Fernando Louro de Sousa, blamed the lack of a strategy of "psychological action and social action" to win the population, "to gain their confidence," as a consequence of which "we now find ourselves in a situation of sending troops and more troops to repress the perhaps irrepressible."[18]

Meanwhile, notwithstanding the favorable developments unfolding in the raging battle of Como, all was not well with the prosecution of the armed struggle. At this early stage, a looming crisis had begun to seriously threaten the achievements of the PAIGC and the prestige of its leadership. Cabral noted that, after only a year of war, "the comrades began not to understand each other, each one on his own, each one abusing, making the abuses he likes in his area, not respecting anyone who goes there as his superior."[19] The chain of command was breaking up and discipline was in disarray. One such "superior" who was "disrespected" when he visited a liberated area (Quitafine) was Luís Cabral, who submitted a scathing report to his brother outlining the terrible behavior of some field commanders, which included "assassinations of men, women, even children, on the accusation of being witches." These acts provoked the "massive exodus of people seeking protection in other areas to escape the abuses and crimes committed."[20] Aristides Pereira, Cabral's deputy, confirmed the "crimes and abuses" committed by the "liberators" against the "liberated," who were increasingly disenchanted with and distrustful of the PAIGC and its leadership.

The successful attacks against the Portuguese colonial forces in the south had emboldened some ethnocentric guerrilla fighters to disobey orders to take the war to the eastern region largely inhabited by the Islamized Fulas. Cabral recounted the defiant cross-questioning by the rebellious guerrillas, mainly Balantas, which seriously undermined the objectives of the armed struggle and years of painstaking preparatory work: "Why should the Balanta go and help to liberate the Fula? Let the Fula do their own work."[21]

Cabral evidently underestimated the depth of ethnic animosity, notwithstanding his political education and mobilization campaigns that emphasized interethnic solidarity. Defiance of the PAIGC's rules of conduct and engagement was facilitated by the autonomy and isolation of field commanders, which is a consequence of the decentralized nature of guerrilla warfare. Ineffective control by the central command in Conakry also encouraged insubordination. During this initial phase of open conflict, Cabral, the multitasking leader, infrequently visited the battlefronts and liberated areas, spending most of his time in Conakry, on diplomatic missions, and at international conferences, to champion the cause of the armed struggle and mobilize vital political, military, and moral support—in addition to coordinating a united anticolonial front representing all the Portuguese African colonies. He would later admit that some of the military commanders "had become too autonomous," resulting in the emergence of "tendencies to self-centered isolation."[22] This unexpected outcome, unanticipated in the various scenarios he had elaborated for the training of guerrilla fighters in Conakry, presented a critical challenge for the PAIGC. In a crucial test of his leadership skills, Cabral had to act promptly and decisively to assert the legitimacy and authority of the liberation movement he led. Thus, the fighters attending the Cassacá Congress would be quickly disarmed and the accused military commanders summoned to appear and respond to charges made against them.

Initially planned as a seminar for the party cadres, Cabral convened what became the first congress of the PAIGC, held on 13–17 March 1964 at Cassacá, a liberated village in the south, as his brother Luís advised, "so that its impact would be greater among our people." Attended by over seventy party cadres, guerrilla fighters, military commanders, political leaders, and village delegates from the liberated areas, the Cassacá Congress addressed the growing political and military crisis, which seriously threatened the very existence of the liberation movement. Cabral astutely recognized that some of the "weaknesses and mistakes" that were "unexpectedly showing up" could become "dangerous for our Party and for our struggle."[23] Besides eroding the support base for the armed struggle, the indiscipline and "criminal behaviors" of the "freedom fighters" also undermined the PAIGC's core principle of civilian control of the military. Outraged by the "abominable crimes being committed in our names" and the resultant "considerable loss of support among the population," Cabral insisted on the precedence and preeminence of politics and accordingly condemned the militarism "which has caused some fighters and even some leaders to forget the fact that we are *armed militants* and not *militarists*" (emphasis in original).[24]

Cabral was dismayed by the cavalier attitude of some of his field commanders who showed up at Cassacá accompanied by several young "wives." One of the commanders even arrived with his *djidiu* (praise singer) extolling his warrior virtues! Among the other alleged crimes were thefts of PAIGC property. Inocêncio Kani, a naval commander and the future assassin of Cabral, was accused of selling a boat engine. The authority of the PAIGC had to be reasserted, discipline restored, and justice seen to be done.

After a lengthy trial, Cabral and the collective leadership moved swiftly to punish the guilty violators: those who were present were immediately apprehended while heavily armed soldiers were sent to arrest those who were absent. Those who resisted arrest, Cabral noted, "were liquidated."[25] Besides executions, the punishments also included demotions and imprisonments. The summary military justice, in the context of a war in its infancy, was deemed imperative. But Cabral would insist on the "rehabilitation" of those fighters found guilty of less serious crimes like theft—including Inocêncio Kani.

The immediate outcome of the Cassacá Congress was the establishment of political control over the military, with the creation of a seven-member War Council, headed by Cabral, as the highest civilian-dominated military organ of the liberation movement. The other members of the War Council included Aristides Pereira, Cabral's brother Luís, Nino Vieira, and Domingos Ramos. In addition to its principal responsibility for conducting the armed struggle, the council also dealt with specialized military training in areas like heavy artillery and antiaircraft weapons. The guerrilla force based on bi-grupos (two-group units of twenty to thirty fighters) was reorganized into a more disciplined People's Revolutionary Armed Forces (FARP) comprising three components: a mobile conventional army, the

Popular Army, responsible for the liberation of the entire country; the Popular Guerrillas, to operate in contested areas; and the Popular Militia, to provide local security in the liberated areas. Political commissars with more seniority were paired with military commanders to ensure the primacy of politics over military matters. Also established was a fifteen-member Political Bureau of the PAIGC, an enlarged Central Committee (expanding from thirty to sixty-five members), and seven departments responsible for areas including the armed forces, security, information and propaganda, economy and finance, and foreign affairs.

With these profound structural changes, Cabral felt it urgent to reassert the authority of the civilian-dominated leadership of the PAIGC, in particular his role as the commander-in-chief: "The leadership of the struggle is the leadership of the Party. Inside the Political Bureau there is a War Council of which I am president as Secretary-General of the Party. There is no important military action in our country that does not pass through my hands."[26] Although this may seem an obsessive need to control, Cabral was in fact emphasizing his responsibilities as the civilian leader of a politicized military at war. Nevertheless, the tension between the "militarists" and the "armed militants" would remain a formidable challenge during the prolonged armed struggle, and after independence the militarization of politics would become a defining characteristic of the new nation of Guinea-Bissau.

Administratively, the liberated areas of the south and the north were divided into regions, sectors, and *tabancas* (villages). It was a pyramidal structure that facilitated communication between the Party Secretariat and the subordinate committees at these various levels. Grassroots participation was guaranteed at the lowest and most basic level, where the five members of the *tabanca* committee, two of whom had to be women, were elected. Cabral recognized the important role of women not only in the liberation struggle but also in the new society being created. Even before the launching of the war, a women's wing of the PAIGC, the Women's Democratic Union (UDEMU), was created in 1961. He acknowledged and promoted the active participation of women in the struggle, in their roles as recruiters, porters, nurses, teachers, frontline fighters, and political and military leaders. The new infrastructure in the liberated areas also included the People's Courts, People's Stores, health clinics and hospitals, and schools.

The PAIGC came out of the Cassacá Congress revitalized and more determined to complete the liberation of the country. The historic event was a critical turning point that set the liberation movement on a more secure road to political and military victory. However, the sensitive and thorny questions of ethnic animosity and anti–Cabo Verdean hostility, both being weaponized by the Portuguese, remained inadequately addressed, even though Cabral was well aware of Portuguese exploitation of "tribal contradictions" and practice of "racism on the basis of lighter skin and darker skin." Thus, the threat of factionalism within the ethnically diversified binational liberation movement remained menacingly real.

Nevertheless, battles had to be fought and the war had to be won. Time was of the essence. Cabral focused on equipping his People's Army with 75mm recoilless rifles, rocket-propelled grenades, small cannons, and bazookas, besides the famous Kalashnikovs (AK-47s). He substantially increased the number of men and women sent abroad for military training, mainly to the USSR, the PRC, Czechoslovakia, East Germany, Hungary, Bulgaria, and Cuba, besides African countries like Algeria, Morocco, Ghana, and the host country (Guinea-Conakry). Maintaining the initiative, Cabral's fighters expanded their operations with the opening of the eastern front, such that by 1966 about 50 percent of the colony and half of its population were under the control of the PAIGC.

Determined to recover lost territory and prove that "Guinea will never cease to be Portuguese," Governor Schulz, a veteran of recent repressive military campaigns against Angolan nationalists, ordered sustained air strikes during his four-year tenure, dropping tons of bombs, including napalm and white phosphorous, "to terrorize the terrorists." A military upsurge swelled the Portuguese army to twenty thousand soldiers, with air power that included helicopter gunships. Commenting on the war plan of the Portuguese, Cabral noted that they "follow the tactics and strategies used by the US and other imperialists."[27] Specifically, he had in mind the ongoing American intervention in Vietnam, on which the Portuguese modelled their colonial war. Like the "strategic hamlets program" of the Americans, Schulz established the *aldeamentos em autodefesa* (self-defense villages), strategically located rural settlements, largely in the eastern region, characterized by barbed wire fencing to "protect" the villagers from "communist influence." The *Tugas*, Cabral elaborated, "used every kind of bomb save the nuclear ones," and maintained that "almost every day, they bomb our villages and try to burn the crops. They are trying to terrorise our people."[28]

Cabral admitted that the Portuguese military upsurge was "generally harder for us," because the high-altitude air strikes targeted civilians of the liberated areas as well as the FARP units operating in contested territory. The impact was devastating and demoralizing, causing huge population displacements that swelled the number of refugees in the neighboring countries. As the indiscriminate bombing raged, the liberators "had the unenviable task of having to explain to villagers fleeing bombardment the need to stay put to continue the war effort."[29]

Nevertheless, Cabral and his War Council pressed on and created mobile antiaircraft units to address the deadly menace of Portuguese air power. Cabral got busy procuring the necessary weaponry and securing the needed specialist training. Cuba, which in August 1963 "said yes, but did nothing" about Cabral's request for military and political training for five of his fighters, turned out to be particularly accommodating.[30] Four months after his meeting with Ernesto "Che" Guevara in Conakry on 12 January 1965, Fidel Castro's government delivered 315 crates of arms, medicine, and food. In July that year, about half a dozen Cabo Verdean militants of the PAIGC, including Pedro Pires and Manuel "Manecas" dos Santos, embarked for military training in Cuba in anticipation of initiating the armed liberation of Cabo Verde. However, following Cabral's decision later that guerrilla warfare was infeasible in the archipelago, all the trained Cabo Verdeans joined the war in Portuguese Guinea.

In January 1966, Cabral himself led a PAIGC delegation to Havana to participate in the first Tricontinental Conference of the Peoples of Asia, Africa, and Latin America, where he presented his critically acclaimed thesis "The Weapon of Theory." Greatly impressed, Fidel Castro promptly agreed to Cabral's request for medical doctors, military instructors, and mechanics to provide the PAIGC an effective logistics capability. Six months later, the Cuban Military Mission in Guinea and Guinea-Bissau (MMCG) arrived in Conakry with thirty-one "advisors": eleven artillery specialists, eight drivers, ten doctors (five surgeons, three clinicians, and two orthopedists), an intelligence officer, and the chief of the mission.[31] The first head of the MMCG, Lieutenant Aurelio Ricardo Artemio, was succeeded in 1967 by Major Víctor Dreke Cruz, an African Cuban veteran of the Cuban Revolution and Che Guevara's most trusted commander, then known as Comandante Moja, during the failed Cuban expedition to the Democratic Republic of the Congo in 1965.

Cuban military advisors, particularly Victor Dreke Cruz, who trained and fought alongside the FARP guerrillas inside Portuguese Guinea, worked very closely with Cabral and his War Council, and the collaboration significantly enhanced the FARP's operational capability. It was Cabral who decided where the Cubans would be deployed, dispatching two groups of six instructors and four doctors to the southern and eastern fronts and leaving the rest in Guinea-Conakry. Once in the war zones, the Cubans found themselves facing the "the impossibility of advising and correcting the tactics of the fight without participating directly in the actions."[32] Aware of Cuban participation in the war against them, the Portuguese were elated when Operation Jove (16–19 November 1969) resulted, two days later, in the capture of wounded Cuban infantry captain Pedro Rodriguez Peralta. The captured Cuban was a valuable trophy for Lisbon's propagandistic equation of her colonial wars with "the war against communism." Peralta was flown to Portugal to serve a five-year prison sentence.

With Cuban technical assistance, the PAIGC attacks on all the war fronts increased significantly. According to Mustafah Dhada, the relentless PAIGC offensive increased "from 112 accountable operations in 1967 to 467 traceable attacks in 1968,"[33] Cabral's fighters were hitting and/or downing Portuguese warplanes and intensifying attacks on garrisons, fortified towns, land convoys, and river patrols. The vulnerability of Schulz's military force was dramatically exposed when Cabral ordered one of his antiaircraft units, led by Andre Gomes, to attack on 28 February 1968 the main Portuguese Air Force base at Bissalanca, just seven kilometers from Bissau, destroying "the control tower of the airport, two airplanes, and three hangars."[34] Schulz ended his four-year term with the PAIGC stronger than when he assumed office.

Cabral's new adversary became General António Ribeiro de Spínola, a cavalry officer who visited the German Sixth Army during its unsuccessful attempt to seize Stalingrad in 1942. Spínola was also a veteran of the Portuguese brutal suppression of the Angolan uprisings in 1961. Recognizing the leadership genius of Cabral and the effectiveness of his army, the new governor assumed office in May 1968 with a declaration that "the war in progress in Guinea is eminently psychological," that it could only be won by "persuasion" and not by "coercion."[35] But his "psycho-social" war to win hearts and minds was not in synchrony with the mindset of his superiors in Lisbon.

Although Salazar was incapacitated by a stroke suffered in September 1968, his replacement, Marcello Caetano, a prominent Estado Novo ideologue and former minister of the colonies (1944–47), also had an incorrigible colonialist bent. Caetano's intolerance of

African nationalism and his profound dislike of nationalist leaders in "Portuguese Africa" manifested itself five months later, on 3 February 1969, with the PIDE's assassination in Dar-es-Salaam, Tanzania, of Eduardo Mondlane, founding president of the Liberation Front of Mozambique (FRELIMO). Eulogizing his "companion in struggle" in his famous lecture on "National Liberation and Culture" at Syracuse University in the United States a year later, Cabral delineated the motive behind Mondlane's assassination to be the fact that "he was able to rediscover his own roots, identify with his people and dedicate himself to the cause of national and social liberation."[36] Contemplating a life trajectory not unlike his, Cabral undoubtedly pondered the possibility of a similar fate awaiting him, and the probability of it visiting him at any time.

Spínola devised a two-pronged strategy to defeat Cabral and his movement by launching a *Guiné Melhor* (Better Guinea) program that exploited the colonially generated antagonisms between Guineans and Cabo Verdeans, gave preferential treatment to the former in the colonial administration, and made notable improvements in the colony's social infrastructure. Spínola also released many imprisoned Guinean nationalists, including PAIGC president Rafael Barbosa, who, in a speech prepared by the PIDE, promised "to be as good a Portuguese as His Excellency." Cabral and his comrades promptly declared him a "traitor." That was the carrot.

In this dual strategy, described by Cabral as "smiles and blood," the stick was the implementation of an aggressive counterinsurgency policy entailing the "Africanization" of the war with the creation of the African Commandos and the African Marines, comprised exclusively of "native Guineans." This was complemented by a troop upsurge of forty thousand soldiers, the intensification of air strikes with continued dropping of napalm and white phosphorus bombs, and helicopterborne assaults.

Although Spínola's Africanization policy was a copy of US president Nixon's "Vietnamization" strategy, the fundamental difference was that the latter was aimed at ending American involvement in an increasingly unpopular conflict, while the former was based in recognition of Portugal's small and overextended armed forces and the imperative to outsource the burden of concurrent fighting in three theaters of war to maintain the *pax lusitana*. The governor's policy reflected a historical trend. The "pacification" of Portuguese Guinea in the early twentieth century was the work of African mercenaries.

Spínola's carrot and stick strategy took almost two years to seriously impact the momentum of Cabral's freedom fighters, who on 5 February 1969 had finally captured the Madina do Boé garrison and who would in 1969 hit twice the number of aircraft (eighteen) than in the previous year. Obeying Cabral's orders to "not let the enemy relax in their barracks . . . not let the colonialist soldier have even one quiet night's sleep in our land,"[37] the FARP conducted some "981 traceable operations in 1970, 300 more than were recorded the year before."[38]

However, Spínola's "psycho-social" war began to produce some of its desired outcomes, including a significant increase in the number of schools, hospitals, and social housing, greater abundance of food in the markets and a wider variety of consumer items in shops, holidays in Portugal for colonial civil servants, and pilgrimages to Mecca and Fatima, respectively, for Muslim and Christian leaders. Together with the intensified air strikes and helicopter-borne attacks, the gains of the liberation struggle came under serious threat. Besides the recently released political prisoners who pledged allegiance to the Portuguese flag, and the increasing

Figure 2. Cabral in pensive mood as the war intensified during the early 1970s. Copyright, Bruna Polimeni (1971), Fondazione Lelio e Lisli Basso.

number of people in the major cities—Bissau, Bolama, Bafatá, Teixeira Pinto (Canchungo), and Nova Lamego (Gabu)—who believed that "independence is unnecessary," Cabral and his comrades also had to deal with the effects of Spínola's counterinsurgency program on the inhabitants of the liberated areas, where the local military commanders "were already losing patience with certain elements of the population they considered traitors, because they gave themselves to the *Tugas* for some trinkets."[39]

To counter the Portuguese propaganda offensive in the "war of the waves," Cabral deployed the PAIGC's new Freedom Radio, broadcasting in Portuguese, French, Crioulu, Fula, Mandinka, and Manjaco, to launch a frontal attack on the belated Portuguese attempts to create a "Better Guinea," underscoring that "*without our struggle, without our Party, the Portuguese colonialists, who have been so long among us without building schools or health centres or housing,* would never bother to do these things (emphasis in original)."[40] Spínola's strategy to win hearts and minds ultimately failed because the overwhelming majority of the beneficiaries of the social dimension of Better Guinea recognized the self-serving nature of the colonial largesse.

Meanwhile, Cabral redoubled his efforts on the diplomatic front, appearing before the Subcommittee on Africa of the US House Committee on Foreign Affairs, chaired by the African American congressman Charles Diggs Jr., where, in spite of the Nixon administration's undisguised support of the Lisbon regime, critical voices echoing American opposition to Portuguese colonialism were still heard. Cabral showed graphic pictures of victims of napalm bombs supplied to the Portuguese by the United States, to the outrage of some committee members, including Diggs. A few months later, on 27–29 June, Cabral participated, together with Agostinho Neto of the MPLA and Marcelino dos Santos of the FRELIMO, in a conference in Rome organized to demonstrate "solidarity with the peoples of the Portuguese colonies" and attended by over 175 organizations from 65 countries. Significantly, at the end of the event he led his comrades to an audience with Pope Paul VI, to whom he gave a dossier on Portugal's violent repression of her colonial subjects. The pontiff told the delegation, "We are on the side of those who suffer. We are for the peace, the freedom, and the national independence of all people, particularly the African peoples."[41]

Pope Paul VI's encounter with the "terrorist leaders" infuriated Prime Minister Caetano, prompting him to declare "the profound regret of the Portuguese Government and Nation" and to recall the Portuguese ambassador to the Holy See. Although he later accepted the Vatican's explanation that there was no political significance to the pope's meeting with Cabral and his comrades, and accordingly restored diplomatic relations with the Holy See, the implicit papal condemnation of Portuguese colonialism was obvious to the world and especially to the people of Catholic Portugal, home of one of the most sacred shrines of Catholicism, the Sanctuary of Fatima. It was a major diplomatic coup for Cabral, who considered the historic audience "a political and moral fact of the greatest importance."

Cabral's "expose and shame" campaign against the Lisbon regime left Portugal increasingly isolated. In Portuguese Guinea, Spínola was becoming increasingly frustrated with the steady gains being made by the *terroristas*. Determined to end the war by "persuasion," the military governor obtained the approval of Caetano to initiate political dialogue with elements of the PAIGC. Exploiting the nativist mantra of *Guiné para os guinéus* (Guinea for the native Guineans), contacts were made and meetings held with some guerrilla field commanders in the northern front. Aware of Spínola's maneuvers and its potentially damaging impact on the cohesion of the liberation movement, the PAIGC leadership abruptly brought an end to the talks when a guerrilla unit ambushed and killed Spínola's negotiating team of three military officers on 20 April 1970. It is not clear whether Cabral knew of or ordered the killing of the Portuguese negotiators, although one historian implicates his brother Luís.[42] The incident left Spínola and the Lisbon authorities furiously vengeful. Considered "Portugal's Vietnam," the "least valuable" of Portuguese colonies had become Caetano's Achilles heel. Given the deteriorating situation, the military governor informed the prime minister of the dire choice they faced: "Either we use all the means at our disposal to eradicate the enemy's sanctuaries or we lose Guinea irrevocably."[43] Caetano accepted the first option.

Spínola took the fight to the PAIGC sanctuary city of Conakry. Operation Green Sea was launched on 22 September 1970, incorporating elements of the Conakry-Guinean opposition movement the Guinean National Liberation Front (FLNG). Closely supervised by Spínola himself and commanded by navy captain Alpoim Calvão, the top-secret seaborne assault by some four hundred mostly black soldiers, half of them FLNG fighters clandestinely trained by the Portuguese on the Bijagós island of Sogá, unexpectedly descended on Conakry but nevertheless met stiff resistance from the Conakry-Guinean forces. The principal objective was to assassinate Cabral and Sékou Touré and install a friendly regime that would expel the PAIGC and the Cubans from the country and effectively end the war.

However, besides rescuing twenty-six Portuguese prisoners of war held by the PAIGC, destroying seven naval boats belonging to the liberation movement and Guinea-Conakry, and killing "over 300 persons," the operation failed to accomplish its primary mission. Cabral and Sékou Touré were still alive, the PAIGC and the Cubans were still operational, and the Conakry regime was still standing. Amid loud condemnations of Portugal around the world, both the Bissau and Lisbon authorities steadfastly denied Portuguese involvement, despite the "smoking gun" evidence of captured soldiers and equipment. The operation's nightmare scenario had become a diplomatic fiasco for Portugal and a boon for the PAIGC and Guinea-Conakry.

Cabral, away in Bulgaria, strongly condemned the invasion. Following the report of a UN fact-finding mission sent to Conakry three days after the aborted invasion, Security Council Resolution 290 (1970), adopted with the abstentions of the United States, the United Kingdom, France, and Spain, reaffirmed "the inalienable right of the people of Angola, Mozambique and Guinea (Bissau) to freedom and independence," condemned Portugal for the aggression, and declared that "the presence of Portuguese colonialism on the African continent is a serious threat to the peace and stability of independent African States." Predictably, the OAU extraordinary meeting in Lagos, Nigeria, on 11 December also condemned the "treacherous aggression," while individual member states, particularly Algeria, Libya, Nigeria, Tanzania, and Zambia, offered military and financial assistance to Sékou Touré's government. The failed invasion temporarily united the radical Casablanca and moderate Monrovia groups of countries that had contrasting visions of Pan-African unification.[44] The USSR, Cuba, the PRC, and other communist countries denounced the "imperialist aggression." Unpredictably, President Nixon sent a "message of sympathy and support" and an aid package worth $4.7 million to the Conakry authorities.[45] The United Kingdom, France, Italy, and West Germany were not at ease with what was effectively Portugal's Bay of Pigs.

Spínola's strategy ended up boosting political and material support for the PAIGC. It was a propaganda bonanza that Cabral skillfully exploited to show "how desperate the Portuguese are in our country" and to rally further international support to ensure that "the advances made by our struggle are irreversible."[46] Moscow, Beijing, Havana, and Prague substantially increased their technical and military assistance to the PAIGC, while Stockholm and the Nordic governments expanded their humanitarian aid.

In the face of their own mounting frustration, the Lisbon authorities accepted the offer by President Senghor of Senegal to mediate a negotiated settlement of the war with Cabral. The Senegalese leader proposed a cease-fire and joint PAIGC-Portuguese administration of the territory for ten years, followed by a referendum on either independence or full autonomy under Portuguese imperial overlordship. However, after the first meeting between Spínola and Senghor in the Casamance resort town of Cap Skirring in May 1972, Caetano ordered the abandonment of the talks. Pressured by pro-empire diehards and fearful of the domino effect that such "concession" could generate, the prime minister rationalized that "it is preferable to leave Guiné through a military defeat with honour than through an agreement negotiated with terrorists which would point the way to other negotiations [in the other colonies]."[47]

Regardless of Caetano's about-face and Senghor's gross miscalculation in assuming that a neocolonial solution would be acceptable to the PAIGC, Cabral already knew that Portugal was being rapidly overtaken by internal and external developments favorable to his liberation movement, that the march of the liberators was unstoppable, and that the protracted armed struggle was on the cusp of victory. Internally, in spite of Spínola's devastating "smiles and blood" strategy, the FARP fighters continued to hold their ground and to administer the liberated areas, which now covered two-thirds of the territory, and where lengthy elections (31 August–14 October 1972) were being held for a People's National Assembly (ANP) that would soon declare independence.

Externally, in his relentless quest for international legitimacy, Cabral invited the UN Decolonization Committee to visit the liberated areas, an offer which was accepted amid strong objections from Portugal. On 2–8 April 1972, a UN observer team entered the liberated areas in the south. In spite of intensified bombings of the region by the Portuguese Air Force, the team successfully completed its mission. Reporting favorably on their visit, the UN observers underscored the popular support enjoyed by the PAIGC and the socioeconomic wellbeing of the inhabitants. On 13 April 1972, the Decolonization Committee meeting in Conakry declared the PAIGC as "the only and authentic representative" of the people of Portuguese Guinea.

The increasingly favorable international environment was also due to Cabral's skillful use of the media to publicize the cause of the armed struggle, particularly in countries that were Portugal's NATO allies. From the early years of the war, he continually invited a number of journalists, writers, and filmmakers to make eyewitness accounts of the armed struggle in progress. The printed and filmed documentation that raised awareness and galvanized support and sympathy for the PAIGC included books by Basil Davidson (*The Liberation of Guiné*, 1969) and Gérard Chaliand (*Armed Struggle in Africa: With the Guerrillas in "Portuguese" Guinea*, 1969) and documentary films by Mario Marret (*Lala Quema*, 1964), Pierro Nelli (*Labanta Negro!*, 1966), and John Sheppard (*A Group of Terrorists Attacked . . .*, 1968). There were also publications and documentaries made by sympathetic authors and filmmakers on the other side of the Cold War divide. For his own part, Cabral created two regular publications for the dissemination of news and information about the armed struggle: the bulletin *Libertação* and the monthly pamphlet *PAIGC Actualités*. Through such efforts, together with his writings, conference presentations, and public lectures, Cabral was able to effectively pull down the wall of silence built around Portuguese Guinea in particular and the Portuguese African empire in general.

Thus, when a confident Cabral once again addressed the UN Decolonization Committee in October 1972, the PAIGC was recognized not just as the only legitimate liberation movement in Portuguese Guinea but also as the party that would form the government of what would soon be an independent country. "The idea of begging for freedom," he told the Committee, "is incompatible with the dignity and sacred right of our people to be free." Therefore, he insisted, "we reaffirm here our steadfast determination, no matter what sacrifices are involved, to eliminate colonial domination from our country and to win for our people the opportunity to build in peace their progress and happiness."[48] Soon after, a General Assembly resolution of 14 November 1972 granted observer status to the PAIGC, which enabled the representatives of the liberation movement to attend its meetings. The "right of self-determination and independence" was also reaffirmed by the General Assembly and the UN Security Council in November 1972, substantially weakening Portugal's position.

Nevertheless, on the ground and especially from the skies of "Portuguese" Guinea, the *Tugas* remained a menace. With total air supremacy, the Portuguese Air Force continued to rain death and destruction with almost total impunity, while helicopter-borne troops wreaked havoc on "terrorist" villages. In 1972, only two Portuguese bombers and two helicopters were hit and/or downed by PAIGC antiaircraft guns, compared to twenty aircraft in the previous year.[49]

Air attacks were among the most pressing preoccupations for Cabral, who became determined to finally checkmate the Portuguese airpower advantage. In December 1972, while also attending celebrations of the 50th anniversary of the founding of the USSR and being awarded an honorary doctorate in social and political sciences by the Soviet Academy of Sciences, Cabral was able to convince the heretofore reluctant Russians to provide surface-to-air missiles. The PAIGC became the only liberation movement in Africa to possess such hardware. Its deployment three months later was a critical game changer.

Having now outwitted the Portuguese repeatedly, it was a highly confident Cabral who on 31 December 1972, at the stroke of midnight, made the following announcement on the PAIGC's Freedom Radio.

> In the course of this coming year and as soon as it is conveniently possible we shall call a meeting of our People's National Assembly in Guiné, so that it can fulfill the first historic mission incumbent on it: the proclamation of the existence of our state, the creation of an executive for this state and the promulgation of a fundamental law—that of the first constitution in our history—which will be the basis of the active existence of our African nation.[50]

Behind the remarkable PAIGC accomplishments was Cabral's effectiveness as a charismatic and visionary leader, shrewd politician, ingenious military strategist, and astute diplomat.

7

Solidarity with "Every Just Cause"

Pan-Africanism and Internationalism
in Action

Driving Cabral's nationalist zeal was an uncompromising Pan-Africanist and internationalist conviction. Although much of his thinking reflects revolutionary nationalism, he nevertheless articulated clear ideas about Pan-African unity and international solidarity. Cabral regarded the armed national liberation struggle in Portuguese Guinea as part of the broader struggle to free Africa from colonialism and neocolonialism, as "one aspect of the general struggle of oppressed peoples against imperialism."[1]

As already seen, Cabral's radical political awakening occurred during his college days in Portugal. He arrived in Lisbon some two weeks after the Fifth Pan-African Congress, held in Manchester, England, in December 1945, had ended with the adoption of two major resolutions addressed to colonized Africans and their European colonizers. Kwame Nkrumah, an organizer of the conference who had recently arrived in England from the United States, prepared the "Declaration to the Colonial Peoples." His mentor, W. E. B. Du Bois, drafted the "Declaration to Colonial Powers." They declared that subjugated Africans had the right to be "free from foreign imperialist control, whether political or economic," and "to elect their own governments, without restrictions from foreign powers"—and advised that, if their European occupiers were "still determined to rule mankind by force, then Africans, as a last resort, may have to appeal to force in the effort to achieve freedom."[2]

Cabral himself first participated in a Pan-African event when he attended the All-African People's Conference in Accra, 8–13 December 1958. At this historic event that was both symbolic and substantive, the host, Prime Minister Kwame Nkrumah, famously declared that his country's newly won independence was "meaningless unless it is linked up with the total liberation of Africa." It is not clear whether Cabral met with Nkrumah during the Accra conference, but he would later develop an enduring personal relationship with the Pan-Africanist champion, who went into exile in Conakry after his overthrow in February 1966. Cabral would regard him as "the head of state in Africa I admired the most." Nkrumah ended his opening speech by assuring delegates of the liberation movements that the independent African nations "stand uncompromisingly behind you in your struggle." When Cabral and his comrades decided to wage armed struggle to end Portuguese colonial domination, the "Spirit of Accra" was stimulative and facilitative.

Cabral went on to attend the 1960 Second All-African People's Conference in Tunis, as a delegate of the Anticolonialist Movement (MAC), and the 1961 Third All-African People's Conference in Cairo, as the leader of the FRAIN delegation. By then, a split had emerged in the Pan-African movement, with the radical Casablanca group of seven countries (Ghana, Guinea-Conakry, Mali, Egypt, Libya, Algeria, and Morocco) favoring accelerated political unification, and the conservative Monrovia group (including Ethiopia, Nigeria, Cameroon, Senegal, Ivory Coast, and Liberia) emphasizing nationalism and interstate cooperation. Cabral, focused on his binationalist imperative of "immediate and total independence," would skilfully manage the tension between the two groups while formulating his own perspective on Pan-Africanism.

As the leader of the FRAIN delegation at the Cairo conference, which was overshadowed by the recent assassinations of African nationalist leaders Félix-Roland Moumié of the Union of the Peoples of Cameroon and Congolese prime minister Patrice Lumumba, Cabral joined the chorus of condemnations denouncing "imperialist machinations." Echoing the opening remarks of host President Gamal Nasser that "many thought imperialism in Africa had ended," Cabral reminded the conference participants to "not forget that not one of our enemies has been really conquered." He urged recognition of the "numerous and great mistakes" in the ongoing liberation struggles, which were not helped by an "African solidarity" characterized by "some hesitation and even improvisation." Cabral further outlined the daunting challenges they faced: the "fascist-colonialist Portuguese" continued to brutally oppress their colonial subjects; the "fascist-racists of South Africa" were daily perfecting "their hateful apparatus of apartheid"; the "Belgians colonialists" had "returned to the Congo"; the "British imperialists" were cleverly manoeuvring to maintain "complete domination" of East Africa and "economic domination" of former West African colonies; the "French imperialists and colonialists" who had recently test-exploded the atomic bomb in the Sahara desert were "killing defenceless people in Algeria" while "increasing their economic domination" over their former territories; and, finally, the "American imperialists," who were "emerging from the shadows and, astonished by the weakness of their partners, are seeking to replace them everywhere."[3]

Determined to broaden the struggle against Portuguese colonialism, Cabral met with his FRAIN comrades in Casablanca on 18 April 1961 and resolved to transform their anticolonial front into the Conference of the Nationalist Organizations of the Portuguese Colonies (CONCP), which now included the Committee for the Liberation of São Tomé and Príncipe (CLSTP). The Liberation Front of Mozambique (FRELIMO) headed by Eduardo Mondlane, which was founded in June 1962 with Cabral's collaboration, also joined the CONCP. While Marcelino dos Santos was the CONCP's first secretary-general, Amílcar Cabral remained its voice and face. He laid the groundwork for the effective mobilization of vital diplomatic and material support for the constituent liberation movements. For example, when in 1970 the Swedish International Development Agency (SIDA) had to decide between the Popular Movement for the Liberation of Angola (MPLA) and the National Front for the Liberation of Angola (FNLA) for its humanitarian support, Cabral's opinion was solicited and he favorably recommended the former. Having developed a close personal relationship with the Swedish Social Democratic Party leader Olof Palme (future two-term prime minister), Cabral was able to leverage the enormous esteem bestowed by Sweden's political class.

Cabral developed a people-centered revolutionary Pan-Africanism that regarded continental unification as a means and not an end. He insisted that African unity was a necessary but insufficient condition for the unification of the continent. "We are," he underscored, "for African unity in favour of African peoples." It was a veiled criticism of state-centric integration as exemplified by the then faltering Ghana-Guinea-Mali Union (1958–63). Declaring the readiness of the PAIGC "to unite with any African people," he stipulated the one condition under which that could happen: "that the gains of our people in the liberation struggle, the economic and social gains, the gains of justice that we pursue and are already achieving little by little, that none of this should be compromised."[4] It was also recognition of the incomplete struggle against colonialism, resulting in "flag independence," that characterized the member states of the recently established Organization of African Unity (OAU).

The magnitude of Cabral's internationalism was reflected in his numerous declarations of commitment to "every just cause in the world," the essence of which was spelt out in a 1968 interview given to *Tricontinental* magazine: "We have as a basic principle the defence of just causes. We are in favour of justice, human progress, the freedom of the people."[5] He expressed strong solidarity with the struggle of the Vietnamese communists against "the most shameful and unjustifiable aggression of the US imperialists." Cabral further elaborated that "the struggle in Vietnam is our own struggle," that at stake in Vietnam was "not only the fate of our own people but also that of all the peoples struggling for their national independence and sovereignty."[6] Perceiving national liberation as essentially a political struggle, Cabral had noted that one of the most important lessons of the French defeat in Vietnam was that politics triumphed over military force: although France still had a large enough army in Vietnam to continue the war in spite of the humiliating defeat at the battle of Dien Bien Phu in 1954, international and domestic pressure nevertheless obliged French withdrawal. Ties between the PAIGC and the Vietnamese were strong enough for Cabral to accept at least two advisors, Tran Hoai-Nam of the Central Committee of the National Liberation

Front of South Vietnam, and Phan Van Tan, a Vietcong military strategist, both of whom Basil Davidson met during his extensive travels in the liberated areas of Portuguese Guinea in the mid-1960s.[7]

To his "brothers" in Cuba, the only country whose offer of fighters he accepted, Cabral emphasized the strong solidarity with "a people that we consider African" because of "the historical, political, and blood ties that unite us."[8] He praised the Cuban people for "defending their fundamental interests" and "deciding their destiny for themselves."[9] At the 1966 Tricontinental Conference in Havana, an international gathering in solidarity with anticolonial and anti-imperial struggles in Africa, Asia, and Latin America, Cabral expressed admiration for "the solidity, strength, maturity and vitality of the Cuban Revolution" and declared that "no power in the world" would be able to destroy it.[10] Fidel Castro, very much impressed by Cabral's "Weapon of Theory" presentation, considered the PAIGC leader as "one of the most lucid and brilliant leaders in Africa," who instilled in him and his comrades "tremendous confidence in the future."[11] The revolutionary solidarity would translate into financial, technical, and military assistance to Cabral's liberation movement, and nine Cubans would die to liberate Portuguese Guinea.

Cabral was also empathetic toward and supportive of the struggles of the peoples of Latin America, who "have suffered enormously," with their independence "a sham" because "governments were created that were

Figure 3. Cabral the consummate freedom advocate: in solidarity "with every just cause." Copyright, Bruna Polimeni (1971), Fondazione Lelio e Lisli Basso.

completely submissive to imperialism, in particular to US imperialism."[12] He was also in solidarity with the Palestinian people, who he believed "have a right to their homeland," and accordingly supported their struggle "to recover their dignity, their independence, their right to live."[13]

Cabral expressed Pan-African solidarity with the struggles of African Americans for civil and political rights, stating in the aftermath of the Watts Rebellion in August 1965, "We are with the blacks of the United States of America, we are with them in the streets of Los Angeles, and when they are deprived of all possibility of life, we suffer with them."[14] Meeting in New York on 20 October 1972 (his last visit to the United States) with some thirty black political organizations, which he described as a "meeting between brothers and sisters trying to reinforce not only our links in blood and in history, but also in aims," he voiced his understanding of "the difficulties you face, the problems you have and your feelings, your revolts, and also your hopes."[15] But he also stated that, more than ties of blood and history, his preferred relationship of solidarity was one of camaraderie, signifying political engagement. Cabral's understanding of the African American situation was also informed by personal interactions with prominent political exiles he met in Africa, including Black Panther leaders Eldridge Cleaver in Algeria and Kwame Ture (formerly Stokely Carmichael) in Guinea-Conakry.

Cabral also expressed Pan-African solidarity with the black people of South Africa where, in the Sharpeville Massacre of March 1960, the apartheid state's police killed 69 people protesting against the requirement to carry a passbook aimed at controlling their freedom of movement, an oppressive system he denounced as a "shameful, vile regime of racial discrimination."[16] To the people of the Democratic Republic of the Congo, where Prime Minister Patrice Lumumba was assassinated on 17 January 1961, Cabral pledged support of their efforts to resist "the aggression of imperialists and the manoeuvres of imperialists."[17]

For Cabral, the flip side of solidarity with "just causes" was the solidarity of people, organizations, and countries with the binational liberation struggle he led and the coalition of anticolonial forces on whose behalf he spoke. The solidarity received in the form of concrete support must be guided by what Cabral called "ethics for aid," emphasizing that it was welcome but it could not be conditional. Such ethics reflected Cabral independence of thought and action, his clarity of purpose, and his stubborn determination to succeed against the odds.

Cabral's frequent absence from Conakry and infrequent visits to the battlefronts and liberated areas of Portuguese Guinea during the early stage of the armed struggle were a significant factor in the indiscipline and crimes committed by some of his commanders and fighters. After the implementation of the structural reforms passed by the inaugural congress of the PAIGC, his numerous essential travels abroad to secure material, diplomatic, and moral support bolstered the confidence and military effectiveness of the liberation fighters. At the same time, Cabral became viewed by the Lisbon authorities as one of Portugal's most dangerous enemies, at the top of the PIDE's list of most wanted *terroristas.*

8

The "Cancer of Betrayal"

The Assassination of Amílcar Cabral,
20 January 1973

Eulogizing Kwame Nkrumah on 13 May 1972, Cabral emphatically declared, "The African peoples and particularly the freedom fighters cannot be fooled. Let no one come and tell us that Nkrumah died from cancer of the throat or any other sickness, No. Nkrumah was killed by the cancer of betrayal."[1] After surviving five assassination attempts, the preeminent Pan-Africanist leader had reportedly died (aged sixty-two) of prostate cancer in Bucharest, Romania, on 27 April 1972. He had been living in exile in Conakry, as honorary copresident of the Republic of Guinea, following his overthrow by a CIA-supported coup d'état on 21 February 1966 while he was on a trip to North Vietnam and the People's Republic of China. Cabral praised Nkrumah for being "an exemplary revolutionary" and a "strategist of genius in the struggle against classic colonialism." He recognized the former Ghanaian leader as a "personal friend" and a "comrade" who always encouraged the PAIGC's war "against the most retrograde of all colonialisms" and duly acknowledged the "practical support" Nkrumah had provided to the liberation movement. Cabral also warned that so long as imperialism existed, "an independent African state must be a liberation movement in power, or it will not be independent." Concerned about counterrevolutionary activities that tended to become malignant, he advised "reinforced vigilance in all fields of the struggle" as "the best homage we can pay to Kwame Nkrumah."[2] In less than a year, Cabral himself would fall victim to the "cancer of betrayal."

As with Nkrumah, there had been several attempts to assassinate Cabral since the early years of the armed struggle. In November 1966 the PIDE reported that an unknown assassin took a shot at Cabral and his brother Luís in Dakar, but both were unharmed. The Portuguese secret police also reported that the following year, in Ziguinchor, capital of the southern Senegalese region of Casamance, Cabral twice escaped the bullets of aspiring assassins. The frustrated attempts to kill Cabral would broaden to include his host, Sékou Touré.

In 1969, a suspicious Cabral prompted the arrest of a man named Jonjon found at the PAIGC headquarters in Conakry with a hand grenade in his pocket, who "allegedly confessed that it was his intention to liquidate Amílcar Cabral in collusion with the paratroopers of Guinea-Conakry who intended to eliminate Sékou Touré and Kwame Nkrumah."[3] As noted in the previous chapter, the principal objective of Operation Green Sea had been to assassinate Cabral and Sékou Touré. This was later confirmed by the operation's commander, Alpoim Calvão, who boldly asserted that if Cabral had been found in Conakry he would have been "surely eliminated." Further proof lies in the fact that Cabral's house was destroyed by heavy shelling.

The concerted attempts to kill Cabral unfolded against a background of assassinations of outspoken anti-imperialist leaders in Africa, including Félix-Roland Moumié of Cameroon (1961), Patrice Lumumba of the DRC (1961), Mehdi Ben Barka of Morocco (1965), and Eduardo Mondlane of Mozambique (1969). Perceiving radical African nationalism and Pan-Africanism as threatening to their economic and strategic interests, the imperialist nations and former colonial powers became determined to maintain control of their African spheres of influence and possessions by any means necessary, including political assassination and direct military intervention. Cabral was well aware that his political commitment, ideological orientation, and "solidarity with every just cause" made him vulnerable to intricate conspiracies, often exploiting existential racial/ethnic tensions, aimed at eliminating him.

Cabral denounced some of the plots to kill him. Notably, in March 1972 he revealed a three-phase "diabolic plan" to kill him and the rest of the top-level PAIGC leadership that had been hatched by the secret police, now renamed the Directorate-General of Security (DGS), some of whose operatives were trained by the CIA during the previous decade "in the modern practices of the fight against subversion."[4] The first phase involved the recruitment of former and current Bissau-Guinean members of the PAIGC hostile to Cabo Verdeans, to exploit grievances and ethnic resentment among the liberation fighters who, as Cabral noted, "due to errors committed and criticisms made against them, are dissatisfied with the current leadership of the Party." In the second phase, the colonial authorities would launch national and international campaigns of disinformation about the breakup of the PAIGC to discredit and delegitimize Cabral and his leadership team and sap the morale of the freedom fighters. Following up, the recruited disaffected elements of the PAIGC would create a "parallel executive" of Cabral's liberation movement that would seek recognition from political parties in neighboring countries and especially from the government of Sékou Touré. In the third and final phase, with recognition and support secured, Cabral and his closest comrades, as well as the loyal militants, would be "physically liquidated." A new leadership would be created "on the basis of racism and, if necessary, tribalism and religious intolerance," and the war would be ended. With the name of the party changed, the new leaders would negotiate with the Lisbon authorities through the mediation of Spínola for the creation of an autonomous "State of Guinea" with "self-determination under the Portuguese flag." Accordingly, all the recruited agents and the leaders of the new party would be rewarded with "high positions in the political life and armed forces of the future State." Cabral added that these agents and their collaborators would also be "well paid for their betrayal."[5]

Assassination as a weapon against political foes was already a well-established practice in twentieth-century Portugal, evidenced by the killing of King Carlos I and Crown Prince Luís Filipe in 1908, President Sidónio Pais in 1918, Prime Minister António Granja in 1921, renowned painter and sculptor José Dias Coelho in 1961, and presidential candidate Humberto Delgado in 1965. Student activist José Ribeiro dos Santos was also a victim of political assassination in 1972. In the Portuguese African colonies, besides the many summary executions and massacres, there were numerous targeted killings of African nationalists, notably the aforementioned FRELIMO leader Eduardo Mondlane.

On the night of 20 January 1973, at 10:30 p.m., Cabral was killed outside his house in the PAIGC headquarters complex in the Minière neighbourhood of Conakry. Returning from a Polish embassy reception accompanied by his wife Ana Maria, he was about to park his Volkswagen Beetle when a stationary military jeep suddenly turned its headlights full-beam on him and his passenger. He stopped, and as he was getting out of the car a group of armed men jumped out of the jeep, rushed over to him, and ordered him to get into their vehicle. Cabral refused. One of the assailants attempted to tie him up with a rope. Cabral indignantly resisted, reminding the aspiring abductors that one of the main reasons for the armed struggle in progress was to end the colonial practice of tying up subject people before meting out brutal punishment.

According to Ana Maria, the sole witness of her husband's murder, Inocêncio Kani, a dismissed naval commander and ex-member of the Executive Council of the Struggle (CEL) who had been demoted, jailed, and pardoned by Cabral for selling an outboard motor in 1971, fired the first shot at point-blank range. The bullet went through Cabral's right side and pierced his liver. As he dropped on the ground bleeding profusely, Cabral, in Ana Maria's account, "still continues to talk, trying to convince them that the *Tugas* were still in our land, and that if problems exist, they should be discussed openly, as is the custom."[6] The impatient Kani then ordered one of his accomplices wielding a machine gun "to finish Cabral." A hail of bullets left Cabral lifeless on the ground. Kani gave orders for Cabral's widow to be taken to the PAIGC hilltop prison known as the *Montanha* (mountain).

Meanwhile, a second group led by Mamadu N'Djai, interim head of security at PAIGC headquarters, stormed into Aristides Pereira's office, tied him up, and bundled him into a jeep driven by Kani to the port of Conakry, where he was transferred to a PAIGC navy speedboat that headed north toward Bissau. A third group led by João Tomás Cabral, an infiltrated PIDE agent, overpowered the guards at the Montanha prison and freed fellow conspirators, including Mamadu (Momo) Touré and Aristides Barbosa, both party militants jailed for nationalist activities in 1962. These coconspirators had been recruited by the PIDE while in prison and were among the ninety-three prisoners released and pardoned by Spínola in August 1969 and then allowed to "escape" from Bissau to rejoin the PAIGC in Conakry—where, after their cover was blown, they were promptly arrested and incarcerated. Numerous high-ranking members of the PAIGC, almost all Cabo Verdean and Bissau-Guinean *mestiços*, were rounded up and imprisoned, including CEL members José Araújo, Vasco Cabral, and António Buscardini.

As Kani sped toward international waters with his prize captive, his boat was spotted by Conakry-Guinean Air Force MIG fighters and intercepted by a Soviet destroyer. With Aristides Pereira rescued and all the other jailed leaders and militants released following the arrest of the conspirators by the Conakry authorities, President Sékou Touré announced Cabral's assassination by the "poisoned hands of imperialism and Portuguese colonialism" through the use of "Africans belonging to the Portuguese colonialist army who had infiltrated the ranks of the PAIGC by pretending to be deserters."[7]

During his exposition of the plot by the DGS to kill him a year before, Cabral had affirmed that, if he were to be killed, "it will be from within our own ranks," that the liberation movement could only be destroyed from within, and that "it will take one of our own to do it." The murderous betrayal was facilitated by Koda

Nabonia, one of Cabral's personal bodyguards, who shared the secretary-general's schedule of activities with his fellow conspirators. Nabonia would commit suicide while in jail awaiting trial. Kani, resentful over his demotion and harboring anti–Cabo Verdean sentiments, was one of Cabral's trusted fighters whom he had sent for training at a naval academy in the Soviet Union and subsequently appointed as the first commander of the PAIGC's burgeoning navy.

A few days after Cabral's death, amid worldwide condemnations of Portugal, the Lisbon authorities responded with predictable denials of involvement, deploying a strategy of deflection with a counter-accusation that President Sékou Touré ordered the assassination as punishment for Cabral's rejection of a proposal for the unification of the two neighboring countries. From Bissau, Spínola also emphatically denied any complicity in the murder, insisting that he needed Cabral as an interlocutor in his quest for a political solution leading to autonomy. Two decades later, the monocled general who tried to kill Cabral in Conakry in November 1970 remained defiant and delusional, maintaining that killing the PAIGC leader was never his plan: "My plan was to integrate him in my government as the secretary-general of Guinea. . . . It would be the glorious end of the war in Guinea."

The condescending racism notwithstanding, Spínola's contention was in fact a total rejection of Cabral's commitment to national liberation. The general was a staunch colonialist who volunteered for a mission to Angola to suppress the 1961 rebellions that initiated the armed struggle there. That the goal of "immediate and total independence" was nonnegotiable for Cabral was never accepted by Spínola, who disingenuously claimed that he "always had in mind a solution that would lead to the self-determination of the people of Guinea," for which "the cooperation of Amílcar Cabral was essential." Cabral's indispensability, Spínola asserted, came from the fact that "there was no substitute in the PAIGC with equal intelligence and *portuguesismo* [Portuguesism, or Portugueseness]."[8]

Yet, while almost all the top colonial administrators and high-ranking military officers in the colony agreed with Spínola's plea of innocence and dismissal of collusion, a few Portuguese officials defiantly spoke out, accusing the DGS of orchestrating the murderous chain of events. Colonel Carlos Fabião, future co-architect of the 25 April 1974 Carnation Revolution (brewed in Bissau) that ended the Estado Novo, affirmed unequivocally, "I have no doubt that it was the PIDE that set up the scheme." Fabião also declared that the Portuguese secret police had previously "tried several times and had failed" to assassinate Cabral and that its motive was "to prevent, or at least delay, the declaration of independence."[9]

Contradicting his initial protestation that he "absolutely [denied] that the death [of Cabral] had been premeditated by the DGS," Deputy-Inspector Fragoso

Allas, head of that secret police organization in Bissau, stated at the end of his mission that "the guys had gone too far, because the mission was to kidnap Amílcar and bring him to Bissau as a hostage. They had not been ordered to liquidate him."[10] Spínola's propaganda officer for the Better Guinea counterinsurgency program, Captain Otelo de Carvalho, another future conspirator of the 25 April revolution, outlined the likely motive for his boss's abduction of Cabral: "the capture of Cabral would give Spínola an enormous shine. It is the typical spirit of the Cavalry: subjugate the adversary, display him as trophy, make him bow, and then negotiate."[11] It was this strategy, the Mozambican-born captain added, that the Portuguese conquistador Mouzinho de Albuquerque used against King Gungunhana of the Gaza Empire (Mozambique) in 1895: capture the enemy, dispatch him to the metropole, and parade him through the streets of the imperial capital. Was this the fate that awaited Cabral had he been abducted?

Cabral's assassination made headlines around the world and provoked a wave of condemnations of the Lisbon regime as well as demonstrations in support of the PAIGC in many countries, including those allied to Portugal. The London *Times* described Cabral as "one of the most extraordinary leaders and thinkers of modern Africa," while the *New York Times* referred to him as "one of the most prominent leaders of the African struggle against white supremacy." In the NATO countries that provided military and technical support to Portugal, as well as in Scandinavia, solidarity groups demonstrated outside Portuguese embassies and consulates.

In the United States, Congressman Charles Diggs, chair of the Subcommittee on Africa of the House Committee on Foreign Affairs, denounced American aid to Portugal and called for an "in-depth investigation under impartial international auspices." Diggs also declared that "the struggle for which Amilcar Cabral dedicated his life—the winning of freedom of the people of Guinea-Bissau and Cape Verde and the throwing out of Portuguese oppression—must go on."[12] The US government condemned the assassination of Cabral but accepted Lisbon's claims of noninvolvement. Yet, a declassified document of the State Department dated 1 February 1973 implicated the Lisbon authorities: "While there is no evidence linking the Portuguese Government directly to the assassination, Lisbon's complicity cannot be ruled out," not least because "the attempted escape of the assassins by sea in the direction of Portuguese Guinea suggests that the Portuguese may have been involved."[13] The US exoneration of Portugal was undoubtedly motivated by Washington's close cooperation with the Lisbon authorities for use of the Azores air base in the context of the Cold War.

In France, the leader of the Socialist Party and future president, François Mitterrand, who met with Cabral in Conakry two months earlier, accused Portugal of complicity by rhetorically asking who the authors of the assassinations of Humberto Delgado and Eduardo

Mondlane were. Among the numerous heads of states and governments worldwide who were outraged by the brutal killing was Prime Minister Olof Palme of Sweden, a close friend of Cabral whose country provided significant humanitarian assistance to the armed struggle he led. Palme echoed the sentiment of hundreds of poignant tributes and eulogies in referring to Cabral as "one of the most impressive personalities I have ever met." At a special session of the UN General Assembly convened on 22 January 1973, where a one-minute silence was observed in memory of Amílcar Cabral, isolated Portugal was strongly condemned for the assassination.

Meanwhile, in Conakry, President Sékou Touré organized and presided over an International Commission of Inquiry, initially comprising leading members of his Democratic Party of Guinea, representatives of the FRELIMO (Samora Machel and Joaquim Chissano were in Conakry on the day Cabral was murdered), and the ambassadors of Algeria and Cuba. Later, the International Commission would comprise seven other Conakry-accredited diplomats, including the envoys of Egypt, Nigeria, Senegal, Tanzania, and Zaire/DRC.

Of the 465 accused persons that appeared before the International Commission, only forty-three were implicated, with nine of them considered active participants in the assassination plot. These suspects were returned to jail and later handed over to the PAIGC following the constitution of its own commission of inquiry. Divided into four groups and tried in the liberated areas, the nine found guilty who included Kani, N'Djai, and Mamadu Touré, were executed by firing squad.[14] The confessions, mostly extracted by torture, directly implicated Spínola, who, exploiting the lingering tension between Cabo Verdeans and Bissau-Guineans, had apparently promised "independence only" following the capture or death of Cabral and the control of the party by *guinéus* (native Guineans of dark skin complexion).

On 2 February 1973, Iva Pinhel Évora attended the funeral service of her assassinated son in Conakry. Before her departure from Bissau, she had a requiem mass said by a priest who was expelled from the colony forthwith, for disobeying the PIDE's order to not mention the name of the deceased "terrorist" during the event. Many guerrilla commanders and fighters also headed to Conakry to attend the funeral ceremony, among them Luís Cabral, Nino Vieira, Pedro Pires, Francisco Mendes, and Carmen Pereira—the only woman member of the CEL, who was in charge of reconstruction in the liberated areas of the south. Also heading to Conakry was Ernestina "Titina" Sila, a member of the Higher Council of the Struggle (CSL) and political commissar in the northern front, who was killed by a Portuguese naval patrol as she crossed the Farim River. Carmen Pereira and Titina Sila were in the first batch of women sent by Cabral to the Soviet Union for training at the beginning of the war. Carmen would later become the vice president of the elected People's National Assembly (ANP) that would convene to proclaim the independence of

Guinea-Bissau eight months after Cabral's death. She would also be the first woman head of state in Africa, albeit for only three days (14–16 May 1984).

According to Carmen, the murder of Cabral "was organized by Spínola" with the complicity of "the comrades": "Cabral died because he had so much trust in his men and did not distrust anyone."[15] In agreement, Cabral's brother Luís affirmed, "My brother's mistake was that he trusted everyone. Without doubt, Amílcar Cabral was not vigilant enough."[16] Not only was trust an important element of Cabral's leadership style, but he also believed in the rehabilitation of sanctioned offenders, hence the amnesties granted to the comrades who fatally betrayed him. Thus, Cabral's humanist ideals facilitated his murder.

Behind the "cancer of betrayal" was the heightened paranoia of the colonial authorities in Lisbon and Bissau with Cabral's announcement of the imminent proclamation of the independence of Guinea-Bissau and its likely domino effect. Notwithstanding Spínola's quest for a negotiated neocolonial solution, his boss, Marcello Caetano, never wavered from his declaration in 1969 that "Portugal cannot cede, cannot compromise, cannot capitulate in the struggle being waged Overseas."[17] And since Cabral was uncompromising on "immediate and total independence," the irreconcilable clash of the logics of domination and liberation made him a disposable enemy, presaged by the assassination of his comrade-in-arms Eduardo Mondlane, and evidenced by the invasion of Conakry in 1970 that failed to "eliminate him."

The funeral ceremony for Cabral, preceded by an international symposium held in the Palace of the People in Conakry the day before, took place at the city's 25,000-seat sports stadium, the Stade du 28 Septembre, where some eighty delegates from around world and the representatives of governments both Western (including the United States, France, West Germany, Italy, and Sweden) and communist (particularly the USSR, Cuba, People's Republic of China, and North Vietnam) joined the thousands of grief-stricken Bissau-Guineans, Cabo Verdeans, and other Africans to pay homage to the man described by the *New York Times* as "the leader of Africa's most successful anticolonialist guerrilla movement." After the two-hour ceremony befitting a head of state, Cabral's remains, in a coffin that had been placed on an artillery carriage drawn by a military truck that circulated the stadium upon its entrance, were deposited in a mausoleum at the Camayenne National Cemetery in Conakry, to be transferred in September 1976 to the Amura Fortress in Bissau.

Portugal steadfastly refused to accept at least moral responsibility for the death of Cabral. Governor Spínola and his close collaborators, especially Fragoso Allas, head of the DGS in Bissau, together with Prime Minister Marcello Caetano and his cabinet, particularly Overseas Minister Joaquim da Silva Cunha, all enjoyed impunity. Spínola returned to a hero's welcome in Portugal and, with the downfall of the Estado Novo, briefly became president of a renascent democracy. He died in 1996 as an "illustrious soldier" promoted to the highest military rank of field marshal, decorated with the highest honor of the Military Order of the Tower and Sword for "valor, loyalty, and merit," and memorialized by the name of an avenue in Lisbon. Overthrown by the 25 April Revolution, Caetano took refuge in Brazil where he died in 1980. Silva Cunha returned to academia as law professor while the whereabouts of Fragoso Allas are unknown.

After more than four decades, postdictatorship Portugal has yet to establish a commission of inquiry to investigate the culpability of Portuguese politicians and colonial officials for the assassination of Cabral, unlike Belgium, which, after four decades of silence, assumed moral responsibility for the murder of Patrice Lumumba. So far it has not been possible to find any archival document in Portugal or Guinea-Bissau showing intention or premeditation by colonial officials or DGS agents to assassinate Cabral. In the turmoil of the 25 April Carnation Revolution, compromising documents disappeared from the archives. It has been observed that "in documentary terms, the assassination of Cabral resembles a shelf filled with ... lacunas."[18] Yet this is similar to what prevailed in nonrevolutionary Belgium, where no incriminating evidence of the murder of Lumumba has yet to be found, but where a conciliatory gesture has also involved the erection of a statute of the Congolese nationalist on a Brussels public square named after him.

While documentary proof of the involvement of colonialist Portugal cannot be found, Cabral's central role in the most intense anticolonial struggle that seriously threatened the dissolution of the Portuguese empire in Africa provides sufficient motive for his assassination, directly or indirectly. In the context of the Cold War, the elimination of Cabral had the tacit support of her NATO allies, principally the United States, the United Kingdom, and France, the major stakeholders who most feared, as in the case of the DRC, the spread of communist influence in Africa. The significance of Cabral in the downfall of the fascist regime in Lisbon and the dissolution of the Portuguese African empire is evidenced by the dramatic developments that unfolded on the battlefields of Portuguese Guinea in the aftermath of his assassination.

A Luta Continua

The Independence of Guinea-Bissau and Cabo Verde, 1973–75

The death of Amílcar Cabral was a devastating blow to the PAIGC, but the tragic loss did not mean that the liberation movement was now a spent force, as the Portuguese had hoped. "The colonialists thought that the death of Cabral was the end of the war," Carmen Pereira recalled, elaborating that, in the aftermath of the tragedy, the *Tugas* launched a propaganda offensive that exhorted the *terroristas* to surrender "because Cabral has died" and everyone else "could be killed in a 24-hour bombardment."[1]

A week after Cabral was buried, members of the Executive Council of the Struggle (CEL) and the Higher Council of the Struggle (CSL) met for three days in Conakry to discuss the future of the armed struggle. An action plan was approved that included the amplification of political mobilization in both Portuguese Guinea and Cabo Verde, the convening of the first session of the People's National Assembly to declare the independence of Guinea-Bissau as envisaged by the fallen leader, the intensification of the armed struggle on all battlefronts, and the boosting of internal security.[2] Aristides Pereira had been chosen as the interim secretary-general of the PAIGC the day after Cabral's funeral. *A luta continua*, the struggle continues.

The renewed resolve of the PAIGC was facilitated by the groundwork laid by Cabral. Believing that he was not indispensable, that if he "died or disappeared, there would be others in the party capable of continuing the struggle," he had devised a practical framework for the implementation of the strategic objectives of the war. Politically and diplomatically, he had successfully established the PAIGC at the international level, not only as the sole and legitimate representative of the people of Portuguese Guinea and Cabo Verde, but also as the party that would form the governments of the two countries, thus significantly undermining the position of Portugal. His assassination only increased the isolation of the intransigent Lisbon regime and galvanized more support for the PAIGC.

Militarily, Cabral left a restructured fighting force, numbering about 7,000 combatants, well trained, sufficiently disciplined, and enormously courageous in the face of a 42,000-strong NATO-supported colonial army with unchallenged air power. Spínola's strategy of "smiles and blood" that killed and horribly burned victims only hardened the morale of the fighters and gave the able-bodied survivors the irresistible urge to actively support the armed struggle. Cabral's acquisition of heavy artillery, including 75 mm and 120 mm antiaircraft guns, and the appropriate training of his fighters for their efficient deployment was supplemented by his procurement of the more effective shoulder-launched surface-to-air missiles, the Strela-2 (also known as SAM-7), from the USSR and the formation of specialist units to employ them.

Cabral's acquisition of the state-of-the-art weapon was communicated to the Lisbon authorities by British intelligence, but while its arrival in Portuguese Guinea was known to the colonial authorities, its nature and functionality was initially an enigma: both the Directorate-General of Security (DGS) in Bissau and the Portuguese Air Force (FAP) in the colony were apparently ignorant of the existence of such a technological innovation. DGS Sub-Inspector Fernando Gaspar admitted that he "did not know of the existence of this type of weapon," while FAP Lieutenant Colonel Artur Batista Beirão acknowledged that "it was a new weapon that we did not know."[3] Cabral, the brilliant strategist of anticolonial subversion, had yet again outsmarted his "superior" adversaries and in the process rendered baseless the racist dogma of General Kaúlza de Arriaga, ultraconservative professor at the Institute of Higher Military Studies in Lisbon and hawkish commander-in-chief of the Portuguese forces in Mozambique (1969–74). In his *Lessons in Strategy for the High Command Course, 1966–67* he declared, "Subversion is a war above all of intelligence. One must be highly intelligent to carry on subversion, not everyone can do it. Now the black people are not highly intelligent, on the contrary, they are the least intelligent of all the peoples in the world."[4]

The renewed post-Cabral FARP offensive was energetic and furious, but contained by his idea of a "clean war." Prisoners of war were to be treated well and civilian casualties avoided. In 1968, Cabral had released two batches of Portuguese prisoners to the Senegalese Red Cross "to rejoin their families and speak to them about us," since "no contradictions exist between the people of Portugal and our people." He further affirmed that "whatever crimes the colonialists may commit, in the future our people will join hands in fraternal collaboration."[5] But such practice was never reciprocated by the colonial forces, which always viewed the freedom fighters as bloodthirsty *terroristas*. "Most acts of terrorism and atrocities," Captain Otelo de Carvalho recalled, "were committed by our forces, not the PAIGC."[6]

A critical turning point signaling the end of Portuguese air supremacy in the territory was reached on 25 March 1973, when a West German–made Italian Fiat G-91 jet fighter-bomber piloted by Lieutenant Miguel Pessoa was downed near the Portuguese fort at Guiledje, in the south, by a heat-seeking Strela-2 missile fired by Domingos Nsali of the new FARP artillery unit Comando Abel Djassi. Pessoa ejected before his aircraft crashed and was later rescued with a broken leg.[7] Under the command of Manuel "Manecas" dos Santos, who underwent specialist training in the USSR, the Abel Djassi unit had become the real game changer. With the Portuguese still unaware of the type of antiaircraft ordnance being used by the FARP, another Fiat G-91 was blown up in the sky on 28 March 1973, killing its pilot, Colonel José Almeida Brito, the operational group commander at the main air base near Bissau. Brito was on a bombing mission near Madina do Boé, the locale that would soon become the birthplace of independent Guinea-Bissau. Announcing the death of Brito, Spínola declared that the plane was "hit by a ground-to-air rocket launched from the Republic of Guinea, while flying over Portuguese territory on a reconnaissance mission."[8] Two North American Harvard T-6 bombers and a French Alouette III helicopter were also hit by surface-to-air missiles by the end of March, but without loss of life.

The first week of April instilled further fear in the FAP pilots of flying the now dangerous skies of Portuguese Guinea. On 6 April, surface-to-air missiles downed and killed the pilots of three aircraft in the north, near the Guidadje fort: a Harvard T-6 bomber piloted by Major Mantovani Filipe and two West German Dornier Do-27 transport planes (carrying a total of five soldiers who were also killed), respectively flown by Baltazar da Silva and António Ferreira.[9] By the end of the month, another Alouette III helicopter was hit by rocket-propelled grenades and light artillery.

In mid-May, a frustrated Spínola complained to his superiors in Lisbon about the imminence of military collapse. The counterinsurgency strategy that depended on air operations was being frustrated as Cabral's fighters wrested the initiative from their enemies. The FAP, which could reach any point in the territory within forty-five minutes, and upon which the colonial soldiers confined to isolated fortifications depended for supplies and air cover, was virtually grounded. The chilling "new reality" facing the FAP, Lieutenant António Graça de Abreu noted in his diary, was that "the PAIGC already has antiaircraft missiles that are effective. The pilots are afraid of flying, who wants to commit suicide?"[10] With roads mined, forts harassed by heavy artillery, ambushes on land patrols, and intensified attacks on river transport, the Portuguese were in dire straits. Morale was dipping as the number of casualties rose. By year's end they would stand at 2,076 soldiers injured and/or killed, almost two-and-a-half times more than in the previous year and "the second highest since the armed struggle had begun."[11]

Sustaining the pressure on the colonial forces, the FARP launched Operation Amílcar Cabral on 18 May 1973, which simultaneously besieged two of the most important Portuguese forts in the territory, Guidadje in the north near the border with Senegal and Guiledje in the south close to the frontier with Guinea-Conakry. These garrisons were pounded with all kinds of artillery including 120 mm mortars and 130 mm field cannons. Both forts endangered the supply routes of the FARP from the neighboring countries. On 23 May, the six hundred and fifty fighters under the command of Nino Vieira launched a massive attack on the Guiledje fort, forcing the overwhelmed force of thirteen hundred Portuguese troops, deprived of reinforcements, vital supplies, and air cover, to abandon the fort in a full-scale evacuation to the nearby Gadamael garrison. During the hasty retreat, twenty-six soldiers were killed and numerous fleeing trucks destroyed.

The fall of Guiledje was a major victory that further emboldened the FARP to lay siege to the Gadamael fort, situated on the bank of the Cacine River, which also fell during the first week of June. The Guidadje garrison was able to withstand the siege with the arrival of Portuguese reinforcements. The impact of the energized attacks by the FARP and the effectiveness of its antiaircraft weaponry had left the colonial soldiers demoralized, prompting the DGS to inform the Lisbon authorities that "the military situation is worsened by the lack of support from the air force, by the terrorist attacks . . . with many weapons and without restrictions to the use of munitions."[12] Indeed, Cabral had amassed a huge arsenal that included armored vehicles and tanks. He had also formed a new air force and sent the first batch of forty fighters for pilot training in the USSR a few months before his assassination, but the FARP air force had yet to be operational.

Meanwhile, on the home front in the metropole, the Estado Novo regime was also under increasing pressure.

By 1973, the colonial wars in Angola, Portuguese Guinea, and Mozambique were absorbing about 50 percent of the national budget and resistance to compulsory four-year military service was causing hundreds of young Portuguese men and women to flee the country. Opposition to the continuation of the wars and demonstrations of support for the liberation movements were also growing. But Prime Minister Caetano remained as stubbornly inflexible as his predecessor, who died on 27 July 1970. A week before the assassination of Cabral, Caetano told his fellow citizens, "We have only one way, defend the Overseas [Provinces]." He would later feel the depth of anger against the Estado Novo regime outside Portugal when he visited the United Kingdom on 15 July 1973, five days after the London *Times* broke the news of the Wiriyamu Massacre in Mozambique seven months earlier, and was greeted by thousands of demonstrators carrying banners and placards denouncing him as a murderer, expressing solidarity with the FRELIMO, MPLA, and PAIGC, and demanding freedom for the peoples of Portugal and the Portuguese African colonies.

With the military balance of power in their favor, the PAIGC leaders convoked the Second Congress of the PAIGC on 18–22 July 1973, at Madina do Boé in the liberated eastern region of the country. Among the significant outcomes of the Congress were the formal elections of Aristides Pereira as the secretary-general and Luís Cabral as the deputy secretary-general of the

PAIGC. The Congress would prepare the inaugural session of the ANP that would formally proclaim the independence of the country, adopt its first constitution, and approve its first government. Another significant development was the creation of two national bodies of the PAIGC, the National Council of Guinea-Bissau and the National Council of Cabo Verde. The splitting of the party reflected the tension between Bissau-Guineans and Cabo Verdeans, aggravated by the assassination of Cabral—a decision that presaged the death of the binational unification upon which the armed struggle was also predicated.

On 8 August 1973, a frustrated Spínola returned to Portugal and was appointed deputy chief of defense staff. His successor, General Bettencourt Rodrigues, arrived in Bissau on 29 August and was briefed on the much weakened Portuguese position, whereby "almost all of the territory of the province constitutes guerrilla area" and FARP forces could "accomplish spectacular actions of terrorism and sabotage at any point."[13] This fragile Portuguese military situation was also the backdrop of the three meetings held in Bissau on 18, 21, and 25 August 1973 by war-fatigued Portuguese "captains" to vent grievances over recent decrees in Lisbon granting conscripted officers the same pay and privileges as their professional counterparts. The junior officers also discussed the prospects of a costly and unwinnable war. Thus was born the "movement of the captains," led by officers like Otelo de Carvalho, who returned to Portugal and, together with some 135 junior officers at a secret meeting in Alcáçovas on 9 September 1973, founded the Armed Forces Movement (MFA). The Movement accepted the radical idea that the end of Portuguese colonialism in Africa was inevitable—a conviction forced, forged, and concretized on the battlefronts of Portuguese Guinea in particular.

On 24 September 1973, eight months and four days after the assassination of Cabral, the ANP held its inaugural session at Madina do Boé, presided by Nino Vieira, who read the proclamation of the new Republic of Guinea-Bissau. The constitution adopted defined the new nation as "a democratic, anti-colonial and anti-imperialist state." A fifteen-member Council of State (including three women) was elected, to be chaired by Luís Cabral, who would be the president of the new republic. Luís Cabral also headed the seventeen-member Council of Commissioners that constituted the leadership of the working government. Francisco "Tchico Te" Mendes was named principal commissioner (prime minister), while Nino Vieira held two portfolios: president of the ANP and commissioner (minister) of the FARP, with Pedro Pires as his deputy.

Although Portuguese troops still occupied the major towns, including the capital Bissau, the PAIGC's unilateral declaration of independence was immediately recognized by over eighty countries and the new state admitted to the Organization of African Unity forthwith. On 22 October 1973, the UN General Assembly adopted a resolution condemning Portugal's continued occupation of independent Guinea-Bissau, followed by formal recognition of that occupation's illegality on 2 November 1973, with seven countries voting against: Portugal, the United States, the United Kingdom, Brazil, Spain, Greece, and South Africa.

Predictably, the reaction of the Lisbon authorities was one of total dismissal. Caetano contemptuously referred to the new nation as "this delirious phantasmagoria that is the State of Guinea-Bissau, without Bissau and without Guinea," with a presumed capital in Conakry, where it could not receive ambassadors "because it does not have the territory to accommodate them."[14] At the same time, the Portuguese soldiers who faced the fire and fury of Cabral's liberation fighters were becoming increasingly disenchanted and conspiratorial.

On 22 February 1974, Spínola's book *Portugal e o futuro* (Portugal and the Future) was published, becoming an instant bestseller. The central thesis was that the colonial wars should end because they were militarily unwinnable and the colonies should be granted "self-determination" within a "Lusitanian Community"—for which he and his boss, General Francisco da Costa Gomes, were promptly dismissed. A matter of weeks later, in the aftermath of the 25 April 1974 Carnation Revolution, Spínola was invited by the MFA to lead the Junta for National Salvation and become head of state, which office he held from May into September of 1974. His advocacy for an end of the colonial wars was the critical factor for his selection over his rival, General Arriaga, who also published a book, in English—*The Portuguese Answer*—in which he defended Portuguese colonialism in Africa as a response to the "strategic-political upheavals" in the world caused by the "neo-racism of the non-white man against the white man," "banditry organized at the international level," and the "Communist neo-imperialism" that was exploiting the first two causal factors in order to take over Africa. Arriaga urged Portugal to remain in Africa as an answer to the communist threat, a message that pleased not only diehard *colonialistas* but the United States and her NATO allies.

Still, during Spínola's brief presidency, secret negotiations for Portugal's recognition of Guinea-Bissau's independence and Cabo Verde's right to independent statehood were initiated. On 16 May 1974, Mário Soares, a long-time antifascist opposition leader of the Portuguese Socialist Party exiled to São Tomé and Príncipe (after several imprisonments in Portugal) by the Estado Novo regime, now foreign minister under the new dispensation, met with Aristides Pereira in Dakar through the mediation of President Senghor. The talks floundered because of Spínola's refusal to recognize the independence of Guinea-Bissau and his insistence on "self-determination" within the Lusitanian Community he had already proposed. However, although Spínola had the support of the MFA that put him in power, there were ideological allies of the PAIGC among some of that movement's leaders, notably Colonel Vasco Gonçalves,

Major Ernesto Melo Atunes, Major Victor Alves, and Captain Otelo de Carvalho. With pressure from the radical faction of the MFA, the secret negotiations resumed in London on 25 May between Portuguese and PAIGC delegations respectively headed by Mário Soares and Pedro Pires. The PAIGC's insistence that Lisbon also transfer power to it in Cabo Verde led to Spínola suspending the talks once again.

Meanwhile, in Bissau, the newly arrived Portuguese governor, Colonel Carlos Fabião, a veteran of "Portugal's Vietnam" and an ideological sympathizer of the PAIGC, reached an agreement for a *modus vivendi* between the two armies. Conscious of the FARP's advantage, Fabião convened a meeting of all Portuguese military officers in the colony, who urged Portugal to remove "all obstacles placed in her path by reactionary and neocolonial forces" and recognize Guinea-Bissau and the right of the people of Cabo Verde to independence. The message resonated well with the key decision-makers in Lisbon. On 18 July, when Colonel Vasco Gonçalves became prime minister of the second provisional government, he declared his commitment to "a just process of decolonization without ambiguities." On 27 July, an outflanked and dejected Spínola announced that Portugal recognized the right of her African colonies to independence and that negotiations for the transfer of power would begin forthwith. Mário Soares and Pedro Pires resumed negotiations in Algiers and reached an agreement on 26 August that recognized Guinea-Bissau and reaffirmed the right of Cabo Verde to independence.

Spínola's capitulation and Portugal's readiness to decolonize marked the climax of the military, political, and diplomatic victories of the PAIGC engineered by Amílcar Cabral. While the MFA played a crucial role in the general's about-face, the submission was undoubtedly the outcome of Cabral's political astuteness and the military prowess of his fighters. As a direct result of the military successes of the PAIGC under Cabral, a month after Spínola took office the MFA-Guiné section had declared that the Portuguese troops, "who were sent to a war that we did not understand or support," had "a unique opportunity to repair the crimes of fascism and colonialism, to set up the basis for a new fraternal cooperation between the peoples of Portugal and Guinea"—if they were capable of "volunteering" their "disinterested collaboration" with the PAIGC.[15]

Portugal formally recognized the independence of Guinea-Bissau on 10 September 1974 and a week later the country became a member of the United Nations, a membership which the United States had conditioned on Portugal's "granting" of independence, a move aimed at placating the Lisbon authorities in return for continued use of the Azores military base. According to declassified documents, Secretary of State Henry Kissinger—who reacted to the PAIGC's unilateral declaration of independence by cynically remarking, "That's really what the world needed, a country called Guinea Bissau"—had insisted two months before the UN vote that the new nation was "not going to be admitted with our vote until the Portuguese have given it independence." The secretary of state had chosen to ignore the fact that Britain's stubborn seven-year refusal to recognize the unilaterally declared independence of the United States did not delegitimize the hard-won sovereignty of the new nation.

In Bissau, preparations for the withdrawal of the Portuguese colonial officials and troops unfolded peacefully, with former foes fraternizing in informal meetings and events like soccer matches. On 13 October, Fabião departed for Lisbon, followed three days later by the embarkation of the last group of Portuguese soldiers. President Luís Cabral and Secretary-General Aristides Pereira triumphantly entered Bissau on 19 October, symbolizing the complete and effective occupation of the new republic. The eleven-year war, in which less than ten thousand freedom fighters inspired and trained by Cabral defeated an army of over fifty thousand Portuguese and African soldiers, was very costly. With four times the proportionate Portuguese troop concentration in Mozambique and eight times that in Angola, the Guinea-Bissau war also brought the most Portuguese casualties—more than two thousand deaths and about four thousand injured veterans. The number of FARP fighters killed is estimated at between one and two thousand for the entire war, while the casualty count for civilian victims is unknown but undoubtedly much higher.[16]

Meanwhile, Pedro Pires headed the PAIGC team that followed up with the process of Portuguese transfer of power in Cabo Verde, a task complicated by the fact that the liberation movement had not engaged in armed struggle in the archipelago and faced a number of rival nationalist groups that were opposed to any form of unification with Guinea-Bissau. Nevertheless, having concentrated its efforts on clandestine political mobilization that produced a solid base of support, the PAIGC leadership, which included Silvino da Luz, Osvaldo Lopes da Silva, and Carlos Reis, was able, through negotiations and the organization of demonstrations and a general strike, to secure the dominance of Cabral's party. With Spínola toppled by left-wing elements of the MFA on 30 September 1974, the decolonization process accelerated. On 18 December, the PAIGC formed a government of transition with Portugal that organized the elections for the archipelago's own People's National Assembly, which, on 5 July 1975, proclaimed the Republic of Cabo Verde. Aristides Pereira became president of the new republic and Pedro Pires his prime minster, both of them leaders of a party now dominant in two sovereign nations.

Thus, the PAIGC's unilateral declaration of independence on 24 September 1973, the result of its military dominance in the battlefield, and Portugal's reluctant acceptance, the outcome of her military defeat, had started the domino effect feared by the Lisbon authorities. In 1975, the Portuguese empire in Africa collapsed completely. In quick succession, the independence of Mozambique (25 June) was followed by that of Cabo Verde (5 July), São Tomé and Príncipe (12 July), and Angola (11 November).

Amílcar Cabral's pivotal role in the liberation of the peoples of Guinea-Bissau and Cabo Verde is evident, but also discernible is the significant part he played in the dismantling of the Portuguese empire in Africa and the emancipation of the people of Portugal from almost five decades of fascist dictatorship.

Cabral ka Muri

The Legacy of Amílcar Cabral

When Luís Cabal's ex-wife, Lucette Cabral, met Nelson Mandela after his release from twenty-seven years of imprisonment, she admiringly told him, "You are the best." Mandela quickly responded, "No, there is Cabral."[1] The humble remark of the freedom fighter who lived to see the triumph of the long struggle he led was a testimonial to the influence of the liberation fighter who did not survive to witness the victorious end of the protracted resistance and military campaign he commanded. The humility of Mandela, who refused to take credit for the ANC's successful antiapartheid struggle, insisting that "it is not the individuals that matter, but the collective," parallels the modesty of Cabral, who always shunned responsibility for the PAIGC's remarkable achievements, emphasizing instead "collective leadership."

More than four decades after his death, Cabral's ideas continue to resonate in Africa and beyond. For his charismatic personality, inspirational leadership, and remarkable accomplishments, he is memorialized within Africa and outside the continent in the naming of academic institutions, government buildings, public squares, streets and avenues, and, in Cabo Verde, an international airport. Although he did not live to accomplish all that he set out to do, his legacy remains inspirational for generations of Africans and non-Africans challenged by deprivation, exploitation, and oppression.

Cabral's assassination marked a definitive moment in the lives of his friends and admirers around the world, but the tragedy was most momentous for his comrades-in-arms. The men and women he inspired went on to defeat Portugal militarily and politically and establish the independence of Guinea-Bissau and Cabo Verde. But the victory was also consequential beyond the borders of these two countries: its ripple effects contributed significantly to transformative developments in Portugal and the rest of her African colonies.

From humble origins in Guinea-Bissau and Cabo Verde, Cabral suffered hardships, witnessed "folk die from flogging" in his *terra natal* and "folk die of hunger" in his *terra ancestral*, and experienced racism as a student and trained agronomist in Portugal. Developing critical consciousness through lived experience and formal education, driven by moral outrage, a desire for social justice, and an indefatigable quest for freedom from foreign domination, he committed himself to fight against the colonial system that nurtured and sustained the enabling environment of exploitation and oppression. Self-emancipation from cultural alienation preceded engagement in the national liberation struggle—which called for the weaponization of culture, since imperialist domination also entails cultural oppression.

Although a Marxist revolutionary theoretician, Cabral was very reticent to call himself a Marxist or communist. He was never an active member of any such organization, but his political thought was shaped by Marxism and his intellectual work was grounded in materialist theory. Nevertheless, he eschewed dogmatism and avoided abstractions devoid of concrete empirical substantiation. He was adamant about contextual specificity. Unlike most other African leaders of liberation movements, he knew his two countries well. Concerned at an early age about the plight of his colonized people, Marxism became attractive to Cabral because it complemented and validated his humanist ideals. More than Marxist formulations, though, his lived experience convinced him of the need to strive to "end the exploitation of man by man."

Important theoretical contributions of Cabral can be found in "A Brief Analysis of the Social Structure in Guinea" (1964), "The Weapon of Theory" (1966), and "National Liberation and Culture" (1970). Motivated by a quest to understand the objective realities of the context-specific environments in which he was politically engaged, he used a Marxist framework that left him questioning and qualifying Marxism. Critiquing the notion of class and the axiom of class struggle as the determinant of historical development, he emphasized the mode of production as the motive force of history and insisted on "the existence of history before the class struggle," so that the colonized would not be left in "the sad position of being peoples without history."[2]

Cabral was a prolific writer. Besides his voluminous studies on agronomy and agriculture, his political works published in English include *Revolution in Guinea: An African People's Struggle* (1969), *The Struggle in Guinea* (1969), *Our People Are Our Mountains: Amílcar Cabral on the Guinean Revolution* (1971), *Return to the Source: Selected Speeches of Amílcar Cabral* (1973), and, posthumously, *Unity and Struggle: Speeches and Writings of Amílcar Cabral* (1975). Although some of his writings can be dismissed as political propaganda in the context of armed struggle and a raging Cold War, there is no doubt as to his intellectual sophistication, which established him among the most original thinkers of the twentieth century.

Cabral's study of the social structure of his country was significant and revelatory. Contrary to Fanon's emphatic assertion that "in the colonial countries the peasantry alone are revolutionary," Cabral underscored that, in the case of Guinea-Bissau, their mobilization was particularly challenging.[3] He delineated the positions of the colonial *petite bourgeoisie*, urban wage-earners, and the *déclassé* (marginalized) in relation to the colonial order, distinguishing between the "heavily committed," the nationalist, and those receptive to the idea of armed struggle. He further noted that the "really *déclassé*" were totally against the struggle, in contradistinction to the role Fanon ascribed to the lumpenproletariat as the "the most radically revolutionary forces of a colonized people."[4] Acknowledging the leadership role of the nationalist petty bourgeoisie in the armed struggle, Cabral emphasized the need for it to "commit suicide as a class" and "be reborn as revolutionary workers" in order to avoid the "betrayal of the objectives of national liberation" and prevent a transition from colonialism to neocolonialism.[5]

Cabral was committed to the establishment of a socialist state in which "revolutionary democracy" would be practiced. By revolutionary democracy he meant the political accountability of leaders, popular participation in decisions that affect lives and livelihoods, the empowerment of the people to escape the vicious circle of poverty, hunger, disease, and ignorance, and the establishment of an efficient economy to fulfill the fundamental aspirations of the citizenry—which he articulated as the desire "to gain material advantages, to be able to live a better life in peace, to see their lives progress and to ensure their children's future."[6] But these aspirations would be challenged by the dilemma faced by the nationalist *petite bourgeoisie* upon capturing state power: ally with imperialism and neocolonialism or ally with the workers and peasants.[7] They would in fact be incapable of committing "suicide as a class" and the process of state construction initiated in the liberated areas of Guinea-Bissau would be arrested after independence, while revolutionary democracy arrived stillborn. The betrayal of the incipient revolution in Guinea-Bissau by its self-seeking leadership mirrors the duplicity of other self-serving leaders in post-independence Africa.

Although Cabral was not doctrinaire, he nevertheless insisted on a solid ideological base for revolutionary action, noting, "If it is true that a revolution can fail, even though it be nurtured on perfectly conceived theories, nobody has yet successfully practiced Revolution without a revolutionary theory."[8] He considered the paucity or lack of ideology as "one of the greatest weaknesses" of the national liberation movements in the struggle against imperialism. This is pertinent to post-independence Africa, where the "ideological deficiency" of governing parties constitutes a major factor in the failure to deliver the promises of independence.

As a revolutionary practitioner, Cabral was a realist and a pragmatist who was against the wholesale transplantation of revolutionary principles and practices, famously reminding the 1966 Tricontinental gathering of fellow revolutionaries in Havana that "however great the similarity between our cases and however identical our enemies, unfortunately or fortunately, national liberation and social revolution are not exportable commodities."[9] He reiterated this point to a meeting of more than one hundred and twenty African-American activists in New York three months before his assassination, underscoring that "revolution or national liberation struggle is like a dress which must be fit to each individual's body."[10] In this he stood in sharp contrast to Che Guevara, to whom he has been likened, and even referred to as "Africa's Guevara." While Guevara believed in exporting revolution, unsuccessfully leading expeditionary forces in the DRC and Bolivia, Cabral's internationalism was limited to strong expressions of solidarity with "all just causes." Ultimately, Cabral remained skeptical of generic prescriptions for revolution, doubting that Guevara's schematization of guerrilla warfare was "absolutely adaptable to our conditions."

Furthermore, while Cabral accepted active Cuban military intervention in support of his liberation movement, he and his War Council were nevertheless fully in charge of strategy. "I would make suggestions to Amílcar," complained Victor Dreke, chief of the Cuban Military Mission in Guinea and Guinea-Bissau (MMCG), "he would listen without saying yes or no, and eventually he made his own decision. Sometimes he followed my advice, sometimes he didn't."[11] The combination of lengthy political preparation of the peasantry and the permanent embedding of his fighters in the rural communities also contrasts sharply with the strategy deployed by Guevara, whose failure in the DRC and ultimate death in Bolivia can be attributable to his ignorance of contextual realities and the disconnect between his fighters and the local rural populations.

Cabral succeeded in establishing the primacy of politics in the armed struggle, although the principle died with his assassination, leaving the FARP playing a central role in the political life of the new nation. He also succeeded in structurally transforming the liberated areas in tandem with the unfolding war, but the profound changes could not survive the post-independence neoliberal structural adjustment of the economy and the liberalization of politics.

Perhaps Cabral's greatest contributions to the success of the liberation struggle in Guinea-Bissau and Cabo Verde were the defining of its aims and objectives and the ensuring of their sustainability throughout the long years of conflict. His modesty, humility, and approachability played a critical role in the transformation of ethnic loyalties and class solidarities into a multi-ethnic movement. He pursued the goals of the liberation struggle with integrity, insisting that his comrades "hide nothing from the masses of our people. Tell no lies. Expose lies whenever they are told. Mask no difficulties, mistakes, failures. Claim no easy victories."[12] Unity and struggle were the essential catchwords. The unity was a work in progress, fragile and vulnerable to manipulations that ultimately fatally victimized him, but strong enough to enable the continuation of the armed struggle to a victorious conclusion.

As a Pan-Africanist, Cabral consistently called for the "total liberation of Africa," for the "economic, social and cultural progress of our peoples," and for "the building of African unity." He was committed to a people-centered unification that would empower ordinary Africans and eliminate the politicization of ethnicity and the ethnicization of politics that negatively impact interethnic and interstate cooperation.

Cabral was a humanist and an idealist, but also a realist and a pragmatist. Cabral the humanist and idealist sometimes clashed with Cabral the realist and pragmatist. He was particularly concerned about the plight of his exploited and oppressed people and deeply committed to their emancipation, which he based on objective realities and pragmatic strategies. He was against gratuitous violence and only accepted the death sentences meted out to his fighters at the Cassacá Congress as a political necessity. As leader of a binational and multiethnic liberation movement, he had to constantly perform delicate balancing acts. A Guinean of Cabo Verdean origin, he was mindful of the negative role of Cabo Verdean colonial officials in Portuguese Guinea and was empathetic to the hostile Guinean sentiments toward them. Nevertheless, he underestimated the depth of the colonially engendered anti–Cabo Verdean grievances and the effectiveness of their exploitation by the Portuguese. Furthermore, he downplayed ethnic hostilities as "secondary contradictions" and underappreciated their profundity among his politically mobilized comrades—which turned out to be a fatal miscalculation.

Consistent with Cabral's concept of total liberation was his commitment to fight against patriarchy and empower women to realize their potential and contribute to national development efforts. Yet, while notable progress was made during the war, the only woman in the first post-independence national governance structure, led by Cabral's brother Luís, was Carmen Pereira, the deputy president of the People's National Assembly (ANP). Francisca Pereira, a war veteran, was also mayor of the city of Bolama. Since then, the proportion of elected women legislators has never surpassed 10 percent, while the number of female appointed government ministers has rarely exceeded five out of an average of twenty-five cabinet members.

Cabral's call for the mental decolonization and "suicide as a class" of the Bissau-Guinean and Cabo Verdean nationalist petty bourgeoisie, in order to identify with "the deepest aspirations of the people," remains pertinent to contemporary Africa. In the post–Cold War context of triumphant neoliberalism, the legacy of his visionary leadership lies in the continued relevance of his progressive ideas. In a globalized world where peoples and nations are left impoverished and marginalized, the fundamental challenge facing the current generation of African leaders remains the establishment of people-centric states that derive their legitimacy from performing functions that consistently and incrementally improve the lives of their citizens. The willingness and readiness of this class to have the political will and moral integrity to undergo the kind of self-transformation Cabral deemed imperative will be a decisive factor in the dismantlement of undemocratic and repressive states that often leave citizens frustrated, humiliated, and desperate.

Notes

Chapter 1: *Terra Natal*

1. Julião Soares Sousa, *Amílcar Cabral (1924–1973): Vida e morte de um revolucionàrio africano*, 2nd ed. (Lisbon: Nova Vega, 2012), 56.

2. Ibid., 54.

3. Juvenal Cabral, *Memórias e reflexões* (1947, author's edition; repr., Praia: Instituto da Biblioteca Nacional, 2002), 17.

4. Ibid., 82.

5. Ibid., 145.

6. Cited in Manuel Brito-Semedo, "Do nativismo ao nacionalismo: A construção da identidade nacional," in *Cabral no cruzamento de épocas: Comunicações e discursos produzidos no II Simpósio Internacional Amílcar Cabral*, ed. Fundação Amílcar Cabral (Praia: Alfa Comunicações, 2005), 330.

7. António Carreira, *Migrações nas Ilhas de Cabo Verde* (Lisbon: Universidade Nova de Lisboa, 1977), 299.

8. Eduíno Brito, *A população de Cabo Verde no século XX* (Lisbon: Agência Geral do Ultramar, 1963), 30.

9. João Augusto Silva, *África: Da vida e do amor na selva* (Lisbon: Edições Momento, 1936), 33.

10. Avelino Teixeira da Mota, *Guiné Portuguesa*, vol. 1 (Lisbon: Agência Geral do Ultramar, 1954), 373.

11. Juvenal Cabral, *Memórias e reflexões*, 164.

12. João Teixeira Pinto, *A ocupação militar da Guiné* (Lisbon: Agência Geral das Colónias, 1936), 202.

13. Luiz Loff de Vasconcellos, cited in Peter Karibe Mendy, *Colonialismo português em África: A tradição da resistência na*

Guiné-Bissau, 1879–1959 (Lisbon: Imprensa Nacional–Casa da Moeda, 1994), 249–50.

14. Juvenal Cabral, cited ibid., 340.

15. Juvenal Cabral to Senhor Inspector das Escolas da Provincia da Guiné, cited ibid., 342.

16. Amílcar Cabral, *Unity and Struggle* (New York: Monthly Review Press, 1979), 243.

17. Juvenal Cabral, *Memórias e reflexões*, 196, 164.

18. Cited in Soares Sousa, *Amílcar Cabral*, 93.

Chapter 2: *Terra Ancestral*

1. Cited in António Carreira, *Cabo Verde: Formação e extinção de uma sociedade escravocrata (1460–1878)* (Bissau: Centro de Estudos da Guiné Portuguesa, 1972), 30.

2. T. Duncan Bentley, *Atlantic Islands: Madeira, the Azores, and the Cape Verdes in Seventeenth-Century Commerce and Navigation* (Chicago: University of Chicago Press, 1972), 235.

3. Amílcar Cabral, foreword to *The Liberation of Guiné: Aspects of an African Revolution*, by Basil Davidson (Harmondsworth, UK: Penguin, 1969), 9.

4. Carreira, *Cabo Verde*, 288.

5. Fundação Mário Soares, *Amílcar Cabral: Sou um simples Africano* (Lisbon: Fundação Mário Soares, 2000), 31.

6. A corruption of the Portuguese word *vadio*, meaning "vagrant," "lazybones"—derogatory terms that in reality reflected passive resistance to callous exploitation.

7. The *bombolom* is a slit-log drum used as a musical instrument as well as a message-transmitting device ("talking drum") by the Manjacos, Pepels, and a few ethnic groups in coastal Guinea-Bissau. Its resonance in Cabo Verde is yet another proof of the historical links between the two countries.

8. Pedro Martins, *The Testimony of a Freedom Fighter*, 3rd rev. ed. (São Vicente, Cape Verde: Gráfica de Mindelo, 2009), 100.

9. Mário de Andrade, *Amilcar Cabral: Essai de biographie politique* (Paris: François Maspero, 1980), 15. António Tomás, *O fazedor de utopias: Uma biografia de Amílcar Cabral*, 2nd ed. (Lisbon: Edições Tinta-da-China, 2008), 52.

10. Julião Soares Sousa, *Amílcar Cabral (1924–1973): Vida e morte de um revolucionàrio africano*, 2nd ed. (Lisbon: Nova Vega, 2012), 70.

11. António Carreira, *Migrações nas Ilhas de Cabo Verde* (Lisbon: Universidade Nova de Lisboa, 1977), calculated from Anexo 1—Quadros estatísticos: Quadro 1. Emigração espontânea, segundo os países ou territórios de destino, nos anos de 1900 a 1952; and Quadro 11, Emigração forçada para o Sul, segundo as ilhas de procedência, nos anos de 1941 a 1970.

12. Amílcar Cabral, *Unity and Struggle* (New York: Monthly Review Press, 1979), 41; Amílcar Cabral, *Revolution in Guinea: An African People's Struggle* (London: Stage 1, 1970), 18.

13. Amílcar Cabral, *Unity and Struggle*, 25–26.

14. Cited in Peter Karibe Mendy, *Colonialismo português em África: A tradição da resistência na Guiné-Bissau, 1879–1959* (Lisbon: Imprensa Nacional–Casa da Moeda, 1994), 317.

15. Cited in Soares Sousa, *Amílcar Cabral*, 75.

16. Amílcar Cabral, *Unity and Struggle*, 56.

17. Ibid.

18. Interview with Colonel Manuel "Manecas" dos Santos, Bissau, 5 January 2016.

19. Amílcar Cabral, "Apontamentos sobre poesia caboverdeana," in *Cabo Verde: Boletim de propaganda e informação* (Praia), 3rd year, no. 28 (1 January 1952): 6.

20. Ibid., 7.

21. Patrick Chabal, *Amílcar Cabral: Revolutionary Leadership and People's War* (New York: Cambridge University Press, 1983), 33.

22. Mário de Andrade, *Amilcar Cabral*, 25.

23. Cited in Archibald Lyall, *Black and White Make Brown: An Account of a Journey to the Cape Verde Islands and Portuguese Guinea* (London: Heinemann, 1938), 98.

24. Cited in Chabal, *Amílcar Cabral*, 34.

Chapter 3: *Mãe Patria*

1. Luís Vaz de Camões (c. 1524–1580), author of the long epic poem *Os Luísadas* (published in 1572) that celebrates

Portugal's voyages of discovery, evangelizing mission, and colonial empire, is considered the country's greatest poet and the father of the Portuguese language, much like the status of William Shakespeare in England and the Anglophone world.

2. Oliveira Martins, "A Civilização Africana," in *Origens do colonialismo português moderno (1822–1891)*, ed. Valentim Alexandre (Lisbon: Sá da Costa, 1979), 213.

3. António Enes, *Moçambique: Relatório apresentado ao governo*, 3rd ed. (1893; repr., Lisbon: Agência Geral das Colónias, 1946), 75.

4. Cited in James Duffy, *Portuguese Africa* (Cambridge: Harvard University Press, 1961), 258.

5. Eduardo da Costa, "Princípios de administração colonial," in *Antologia colonial portuguesa*, vol. 1, *Política e administração* (Lisbon: Agência Geral das Colónias, 1946), 88.

6. Cited in Oleg Ignatiev, *Amílcar Cabral* (Moscow: Edições Progresso, 1984), 15.

7. Cited in Patrick Chabal, *Amílcar Cabral: Revolutionary Leadership and People's War* (New York: Cambridge University Press, 1983), 36.

8. Chabal, *Amílcar Cabral*, 36.

9. Cited in Mário de Andrade, *Amilcar Cabral: Essai de biographie politique* (Paris: François Maspero, 1980), 30.

10. Cited in Andrade, *Amílcar Cabral*, 32.

11. Cited in Julião Soares Sousa, *Amílcar Cabral (1924–1973): Vida e morte de um revolucionàrio africano*, 2nd ed. (Lisbon: Nova Vega, 2012), 129.

12. Cited in Daniel dos Santos, *Amílcar Cabral: Um outro olhar* (Lisbon: Chiado Editora, 2014), 79.

13. Cited in Andrade, *Amílcar Cabral*, 33.

14. Mário de Andrade, cited in Tomás Medeiros, *A verdadeira morte de Amílcar Cabral* (Lisbon: Althum, 2012), 43.

15. Amílcar Cabral, *Unity and Struggle* (New York: Monthly Review Press, 1979), 143.

16. Mário de Andrade, cited in Chabal, *Amílcar Cabral*, 45.

17. Cited ibid.

18. Amílcar Cabral to Maria Helena Rodrigues, 17 September 1952, in Iva Cabral, Márcia Souto, and Filinto Elísio,

eds., *Cartas de Amílcar Cabral a Maria Helena: A outra face do homem* (Lisbon: Rosa de Porcelana, 2016), 338.

Chapter 4: Return to *Terra Natal*

1. Amílcar Cabral to Maria Helena Rodrigues, 24 September 1952, in *Cartas de Amílcar Cabral a Maria Helena: A outra face do homem,* ed. Iva Cabral, Márcia Souto, and Filinto Elísio (Lisbon: Rosa de Porcelana, 2016), 348.

2. Cited in Patrick Chabal, *Amílcar Cabral: Revolutionary Leadership and People's War* (New York: Cambridge University Press, 1983), 36.

3. Cited in "Speech by the Prime Minister of Ghana at the opening session of the All-African People's Conference, on Monday, December 8, 1958," http://www.columbia.edu/itc/history/mann/w3005/nkrumba.html.

4. Cited in Modern History Sourcebook, "All-African People's Conference: Resolution on Imperialism and Colonialism, Accra, December 5–13, 1958," https://sourcebooks.fordham.edu/mod/1958-aapc-res1.asp.

5. Cited in Peter Karibe Mendy, *Colonialismo português em África: A tradição da resistência na Guiné-Bissau, 1879–1959* (Lisbon/Bissau: Imprensa Nacional–Casa da Moeda/Instituto Nacional de Estudos e Pesquisa, 1994), 342.

6. Amílcar Cabral, *Revolution in Guinea: An African People's Struggle* (London: Stage 1, 1970), 25.

7. Cited in Daniel dos Santos, *Amílcar Cabral: Um outro olhar* (Lisbon: Chiado Editora, 2014), 124.

8. Amílcar Cabral, *Unity and Struggle* (New York: Monthly Review Press, 1979), 145.

9. Amílcar Cabral, *Revolution in Guinea,* 50–51.

10. Discussed in chapter 10, on the legacy of Amílcar Cabral.

11. Mendy, *Colonialismo português em África,* 311.

12. Interview with Guinea-Bissau War of Independence veteran Carmen Pereira, Bissau, 12 January 2016.

13. Amílcar Cabral, *Unity and Struggle,* 35.

14. Dalila Cabrita Mateus, *A PIDE/DGS na guerra colonial (1961–1974)* (Lisbon: Terramar, 2004), 30.

15. Amílcar Cabral, "Posto Agrícola Experimental dos Serviços Agrícolas e Florestais: Boletim informativo no. 1," *Ecos da Guiné* 3, no. 30 (January 1953): 25.

16. Ibid.

17. Governor Jorge Frederico Velez Caroço, cited in Mendy, *Colonialismo português em África*, 351.

18. Amílcar Cabral, *Revolution in Guinea*, 28.

19. Cited in Mário de Andrade, "Biographical Notes," in Amílcar Cabral, *Unity and Struggle*, xv.

20. Cited in Julião Soares Sousa, *Amílcar Cabral (1924–1973): Vida e morte de um revolucionàrio africano*, 2nd ed. (Lisbon: Nova Vega, 2012), 175.

21. Amílcar Cabral, *Unity and Struggle*, 29.

22. Cited in Soares Sousa, *Amílcar Cabral*, 180–81.

23. Soares Sousa, *Amílcar Cabral*, 181.

24. Cited in Soares Sousa, *Amílcar Cabral*, 181.

25. Ário Lobo de Azevedo, "A propósito da dimensão humana de Amílcar Cabral," in Amílcar Cabral, *Estudos agrários de Amílcar Cabral* (Lisbon/Bissau: Instituto de Investigação Cientifica Tropical/Instituto Nacional de Estudos e Pesquisa, 1988), 11.

26. Amílcar Cabral to Maria Helena Rodrigues, 30 August 1955, in Cabral, Souto, and Elísio, *Cartas de Amílcar Cabral a Maria Helena*, 365.

27. Lúcio Lara, *Um amplo movimento: Itinerário do MPLA através de documentos e anotações*, vol. 1 (Luanda: Edição Lúcio e Ruth Lara, 1998), 26.

28. Soares Sousa, *Amílcar Cabral*, 184–86.

29. Mário de Andrade, "Biographical Notes," in Amílcar Cabral, *Unity and Struggle*, xxvii.

30. Aristides Pereira, *Uma luta, um partido, dois países: Guiné-Bissau e Cabo Verde* (Lisbon: Editorial Notícias, 2002), 85.

31. Amílcar Cabral, cited in Pereira, *Uma luta, um partido, dois países*, 86–87.

Chapter 5: Binationalism in Action

1. Editorial, "Modern Culture and Our Destiny," *Présence africaine*, nos. 8–9–10 (June–November 1956): 6.

2. Quoted in Claude Wauthier, *The Literature and Thought of Modern Africa: A Survey*, 2nd Eng. lang. ed. (London: Heinemann Educational, 1978), 19.

3. Lúcio Lara, *Um amplo movimento: Itinerário do MPLA através de documentos e anotações*, vol. 1 (Luanda: Edição Lúcio e Ruth Lara, 1998), 39.

4. Ibid., 59.

5. Amílcar Cabral, "Relatório de Amílcar Cabral," in Lara, *Um amplo movimento*, 98–99.

6. Ibid., 99.

7. Amílcar Cabral, "Carta de Amilcar Cabral," in Lara, *Um amplo movimento*, 104.

8. Aristides Pereira, *Uma luta, um partido, dois países: Guiné-Bissau e Cabo Verde* (Lisbon: Editorial Notícias, 2002), 86; and Luís Cabral, *Cronica de Libertação* (Lisbon: O Jornal, 1984), 69.

9. Daniel dos Santos, *Amílcar Cabral: Um outro olhar* (Lisbon: Chiado Editora), 167.

10. Amílcar Cabral, "Carta de Amílcar Cabral," in Lara, *Um amplo movimento*, 104.

11. Cited in Basil Davidson, *The Liberation of Guiné: Aspects of an African Revolution* (Harmondsworth, UK: Penguin, 1969), 32.

12. Amílcar Cabral, *Revolution in Guinea*, 31.

13. "Carta de Amílcar Cabral," in Lara, *Um amplo movimento*, 105.

14. Ibid.

15. "Memorandum de Amílcar Cabral e Mário de Andrade," in Lara, *Um amplo movimento*, 234.

16. Cited in "Carta da FRAIN," in Lara, *Um amplo movimento*, 247.

17. "Relatório de Amílcar Cabral," in Lara, *Um amplo movimento*, 98.

18. This and following quotations from Amílcar Cabral, *Unity and Struggle* (New York: Monthly Review Press, 1979), 17, 27, reprinting the pamphlet Amílcar Cabral [Abel Djassi, pseud.], *The Facts about Portugal's African Colonies* (London: Union of Democratic Control, 1961).

19. Amílcar Cabral, *Revolution in Guinea: An African People's Struggle* (London: Stage 1, 1970), 128.

20. Cited in Aristides Pereira, *Uma luta, um partido, dois países*, 145.

21. Amílcar Cabral, cited in Patrick Chabal, *Amílcar Cabral: Revolutionary Leadership and People's War* (New York: Cambridge University Press, 1983), 66.

22. Amílcar Cabral, *Revolution in Guinea*, 111.

23. Amílcar Cabral, *Unity and Struggle*, 75.

24. Amílcar Cabral, *Revolution in Guinea*, 83.

25. Ibid., 87.

Chapter 6: Conducting Armed Struggle

1. "*Tugas*" was a local name for the Portuguese colonialists.

2. Quotations in this paragraph in Aristides Pereira, *Uma luta, um partido, dois países: Guiné-Bissau e Cabo Verde* (Lisbon: Editorial Notícias, 2002), 141.

3. Amílcar Cabral, *Revolution in Guinea: An African People's Struggle* (London: Stage 1, 1970), 63–64.

4. Cited in Basil Davidson, *The Liberation of Guiné: Aspects of an African Revolution* (Harmondsworth, UK: Penguin, 1969), 97.

5. Amílcar Cabral, *Revolution in Guinea*, 36.

6. Cited in Julião Soares Sousa, *Amílcar Cabral (1924–1973): Vida e morte de um revolucionàrio africano*, 2nd ed. (Lisbon: Nova Vega, 2012), 352.

7. Amílcar Cabral, foreword to *The Liberation of Guiné: Aspects of an African Revolution*, by Basil Davidson (Harmondsworth, UK: Penguin, 1969), 14.

8. Amílcar Cabral, *Unity and Struggle* (New York: Monthly Review Press, 1979), 173.

9. A. Costa Pereira, "Apontamentos sobre a política da Guiné Portuguesa e territórios vizinhos," report of the Polícia Internacional e de Defesa do Estado (PIDE), 17 January 1963, available at Casa comum (Fundação Mário Soares), http://casacomum.org/cc/visualizador?pasta=04999.015.

10. António Augusto Peixoto Correia, "Aos propósitos do invasores," *O arauto. Diário da Guiné Portuguesa*, 19th year, no. 4527, 1 August 1961.

11. Cited in Dalila Cabrita Mateus, *A PIDE/DGS na guerra colonial (1961–1974)* (Lisbon: Terramar, 2004), 99.

12. Costa Pereira, "Apontamentos Sobre a Politica."

13. Aristides Pereira, *Uma luta, um partido, dois países,* 145.

14. Costa Pereira, "Apontamentos Sobre a Politica."

15. Ibid.

16. Amílcar Cabral, cited in Daniel dos Santos, *Amílcar Cabral: Um outro olhar* (Lisbon: Chiado Editora, 2014), 324.

17. Amílcar Cabral, *Unity and Struggle* (New York: Monthly Review Press, 1979), 176.

18. Cited in José Matos, "O inicio da guerra na Guiné (1961–1964)," *Revista militar,* no. 2566 (November 2015), https://www.revistamilitar.pt/artigo/1066.

19. Cited in Santos, *Amílcar Cabral,* 362.

20. Luís Cabral, *Crónica da libertação* (Lisbon: O Jornal, 1984), 158.

21. Amílcar Cabral, cited in Basil Davidson, *The Liberation of Guiné: Aspects of an African Revolution* (Harmondsworth, UK: Penguin, 1969), 102.

22. Cited in Patrick Chabal, *Amílcar Cabral: Revolutionary Leadership and People's War* (New York: Cambridge University Press, 1983), 78.

23. Amílcar Cabral, *Unity and Struggle,* 177.

24. Amílcar Cabral, *Revolution in Guinea,* 70.

25. Cited in Chabal, *Amílcar Cabral,* 79.

26. Amílcar Cabral, *Revolution in Guinea,* 131.

27. Ibid., 112.

28. Ibid., 112, 113.

29. Mustafah Dhada, *Warriors at Work: How Guinea Was Really Set Free* (Niwot: University Press of Colorado), 34.

30. "Said yes, but did nothing" is Piero Gleijeses's phrase, in his "The First Ambassadors: Cuba's Contribution to Guinea-Bissau's War of Independence," *Journal of Latin American Studies* 29, no. 1 (February 1997): 47.

31. Ibid., 51.

32. Oscar Oramas, *Amílcar Cabral: Para além do seu tempo* (Lisbon: Hugin Editores, 1998), 82.

33. Dhada, *Warriors at Work,* 35.

34. PAIGC, "Communique of the Political Bureau," cited in Santos, *Amílcar Cabral*, 387.

35. António de Spínola, *Por uma Guiné melhor* (Lisbon: Agência Geral do Ultramar, 1970), 138.

36. Amílcar Cabral, *Unity and Struggle*, 139.

37. Ibid., 231.

38. Dhada, *Warriors at Work*, 43.

39. Pereira, *Uma luta, um partido, dois países*, 192.

40. Amílcar Cabral, *Unity and Struggle*, 191.

41. Cited in R. A. H. Robinson, *Contemporary Portugal: A History* (London: George Allen and Unwin, 1979), 179.

42. Santos, *Amílcar Cabral*, 393–99.

43. Cited in Gleijeses, "First Ambassadors," 57.

44. Following the 1958 All African People's Conference held in Accra, two main groups of independent African nations emerged with opposing visions of Pan-African unification: a small Casablanca group (Ghana, Guinea, Mali, the United Arab Republic, and Morocco, plus the Provisional Government of Algeria), formed in Casablanca in January 1961, which championed immediate continental unification; and a larger Monrovia group (including Nigeria, Liberia, Ivory Coast, Senegal, Cameroon, Ethiopia, Somalia, Tunisia, and the Malagasy Republic), created in Monrovia in May 1961, which advocated a gradualist approach. The establishment of the Organization of African Unity on 25 May 1963 was a compromise between these two groups. See chapter 7 for Cabral's position on Pan-African unity.

45. Keesing's, "Repulse of Raids by 'Mercenaries' and Guinean Exiles," *Keesing's Contemporary Archives* 17 (December 1970): 24353, http://web.stanford.edu/group/tomzgroup /pmwiki/uploads/1385-Keesings-1970-12-a-RRW.pdf.

46. Amílcar Cabral, *Unity and Struggle*, 204

47. Cited in Norrie MacQueen, "Portugal's First Domino: 'Pluricontinentalism' and Colonial War in Guiné-Bissau, 1963–1974," *Contemporary European History* 8, no. 2 (July 1999): 221.

48. Cited by Mário de Andrade, "Biographical Notes," in Amílcar Cabral, *Unity and Struggle*, xxx.

49. Dhada, *Warriors at Work*, 171.

50. Cited in Lars Rudebeck, "Reading Cabral on Democracy," in *Africa's Contemporary Challenges: The Legacy of Amilcar Cabral*, ed. Carlos Lopes (New York: Routledge, 2010), 88–89.

Chapter 7: Solidarity with "Every Just Cause"

1. Amílcar Cabral, *Unity and Struggle* (New York: Monthly Review Press, 1979), 253.

2. Cited in J. Ayodele Langley, *Pan-Africanism and Nationalism in West Africa, 1900–1945: A Study in Ideology and Social Classes* (Oxford: Clarendon, 1973), 354–55.

3. Amílcar Cabral, *Revolution in Guinea: An African People's Struggle* (London: Stage 1, 1970), 14–15.

4. Amílcar Cabral, *Unity and Struggle*, 254.

5. Amílcar Cabral, *Revolution in Guinea*, 120.

6. Ibid., 66, 121.

7. Basil Davidson, *The Liberation of Guiné: Aspects of an African Revolution* (Harmondsworth, UK: Penguin, 1969), 16, 18.

8. Amílcar Cabral, *Revolution in Guinea*, 120.

9. Ibid., 66.

10. Amílcar Cabral, "The Weapon of Theory." Address to the first Tricontinental Conference of the Peoples of Asia, Africa, and Latin America, Havana, 3 January 1966," https://www.marxists.org/subject/africa/cabral/1966/weapon-theory.htm.

11. Fidel Castro, Speech at the Closing Session of the Tricontinental Conference, Havana, 16 January 1966, https://www.marxists.org/history/cuba/archive/castro/1966/01/15.htm.

12. Amílcar Cabral, *Revolution in Guinea*, 121.

13. Ibid., 120.

14. Ibid., 66.

15. Amílcar Cabral, *Return to the Source: Selected Speeches of Amilcar Cabral* (New York: Monthly Review Press, 1973), 75, 92.

16. Amílcar Cabral, *Unity and Struggle*, 255.

17. Ibid.

1. Amílcar Cabral, *Unity and Struggle* (New York: Monthly Review Press, 1979), 117.

2. Ibid., 114–17.

3. Julião Soares Sousa, *Amílcar Cabral (1924–1973): Vida e morte de um revolucionàrio africano*, 2nd ed. (Lisbon: Nova Vega, 2012), 404.

4. Jack Bourderie, "A Tough Little Monkey," in *Dirty Work 2: The CIA in Africa*, ed. Ellen Ray et al. (London: Zed, 1982), 183.

5. Citations from excerpt in Leopoldo Amado, *Guerra colonial e guerra de libertação nacional, 1950–1974: O caso da Guiné-Bissau* (Lisbon: IPAD, 2011), 325.

6. Cited in ibid., 330.

7. Cited in Bruno Crimi, "Les assassins de Cabral," *Jeune Afrique*, 3 February 1973, 8–12, available at *Casa comum* (Fundação Mário Soares, Documentos Amílcar Cabral), http://casacomum.org/cc/visualizador?pasta=07701.005.

8. Antonio de Spínola, interview with José Pedro Castanheiro, first published in two articles in *Expresso* (Lisbon) on 16 January 1993 and 30 April 1994; cited in José Pedro Castanheira, *Quem mandou matar Amílcar Cabral?* (Lisbon: Relógio d'Água, 1995), 232.

9. Cited in Castanheira, *Quem mandou matar Amílcar Cabral?*, 222.

10. Cited in ibid., 225.

11. Cited in ibid., 212.

12. Charles Diggs, text quoted in "Tributes to a Fallen Comrade," *Ufahamu: A Journal of African Studies* 3, no. 3 (Winter 1973): 15, http://escholarship.org/uc/item/4vf0v6ws.

13. Cited in US Department of State, "Portuguese Guinea: The PAIGC after Amilcar Cabral" (Declassified PA/HO Department of State E.O. 12958), https://2001-2009.state.gov/documents/organization/67534.pdf

14. Oleg Ignatiev. *Três tiros da PIDE. Quem, porque e como mataram Amílcar Cabral* (Lisbon: Prelo Editora, 1975), 185.

15. Carmen Maria de Araújo Pereira, *Os meus três amores* (Bissau: Instituto Nacional de Estudos e Pesquisa, 2016), 162.

16. Cited in Castanheira, *Quem mandou matar Amílcar Cabral?*, 81.

17. Marcello Caetano, *Portugal não pode ceder: Discurso pronunciado no Palácio das Necessidades em 6 de Outubro de 1969* (Lisbon: Secretaria de Estado de Informação e Turismo, 1969).

18. Castanheira, *Quem mandou matar Amílcar Cabral?*, 229.

Chapter 9: *A Luta Continua*

1. Carmen Maria de Araújo Pereira, *Os meus três amores* (Bissau: Instituto Nacional de Estudos e Pesquisa, 2016), 162.

2. Partido Africano da Independência da Guiné e Cabo Verde, "*Sobre o cobarde e criminoso assassinato do nosso querido leader, Amílcar Cabral, fundador e secretario geral do PAIGC: Decisões da direcção do partido*" (Conakry: PAIGC, 1973).

3. Cited in José Pedro Castanheira, *Quem mandou matar Amílcar Cabral?* (Lisbon: Relógio d'Água, 1995), 214.

4. Cited in Amílcar Cabral, *Unity and Struggle* (New York: Monthly Review Press, 1979), 214.

5. Amílcar Cabral, *Revolution in Guinea: An African People's Struggle* (London: Stage 1, 1970), 125.

6. Cited in Patrick Chabal, *Amílcar Cabral: Revolutionary Leadership and People's War* (New York: Cambridge University Press, 1983), 148.

7. J. Pinto Ferreira and Miguel Pessoa, "Guiné 63/74–P3859: FAP (6): A Introdução do míssil russo SAM-7 Strela no CTIG," *Luís Graça & camaradas da Guiné* (blog), 9 February 2009, https://blogueforanadaevaotres.blogspot.com/2009/02/guine-6374-p3859-fap-6-introducao-do.html.

8. Ibid.

9. António da Graça Abreu and Luís Graça, "Guiné 63/74–P1668: In memoriam do piloto aviador Baltazar da Silva e de outros portugueses com asas de pássaro (António da Graça Abreu / Luís Graça)," *Luís Graça & Camaradas da Guiné* (blog), 17 April 2007, https://blogueforanadaevaotres.blogspot.com/2007/04/guin-6374-p1669-in-memoriam-do-piloto.html.

10. Ibid.

11. Mustafah Dhada, *Warriors at Work: How Guinea Was Really Set Free* (Niwot: University Press of Colorado, 1993), 52.

12. Cited in Leopoldo Amado, *Guerra colonial e guerra de libertação nacional, 1950–1974: O caso da Guiné-Bissau* (Lisbon: IPAD, 2011), 343.

13. Cited in Castanheira, *Quem mandou matar Amílcar Cabral?*, 215.

14. Marcello Caetano, *Depoimento* (Rio de Janeiro: Distribuidora Record, 1974), 225.

15. Cited in Chabal, *Amílcar Cabral,* 150.

16. Ibid., 102.

Chapter 10: *Cabral ka Muri*

1. Cited in Gérard Chaliand, *La pointe du couteau: Mémoires* (Paris: Robert Laffont, 2011), Kindle edition, "Amilcar Cabral et le marquis de Guinée-Bissau," Location 4246 of 7483.

2. Amílcar Cabral, *Unity and Struggle* (New York: Monthly Review Press, 1979), 125.

3. Frantz Fanon, *The Wretched of the Earth* (Harmondsworth, England: Penguin, 1967), 47.

4. Ibid., 103.

5. Amílcar Cabral, *Revolution in Guinea: An African People's Struggle* (London: Stage 1, 1969), 89.

6. Amílcar Cabral, *Unity and Struggle,* 241.

7. Amílcar Cabral, *Revolution in Guinea,* 57.

8. Amílcar Cabral, *Unity and Struggle,* 123.

9. Ibid.

10. Amílcar Cabral, *Return to the Source: Selected Speeches of Amilcar Cabral* (New York: Monthly Review Press, 1973), 77.

11. Cited in Piero Gleijeses, "The First Ambassadors: Cuba's Contribution to Guinea-Bissau's War of Independence," *Journal of Latin American Studies* 29, no. 1 (February 1997): 63.

12. Amílcar Cabral, *Revolution in Guinea,* 72.

Bibliography

Alexandre, Valentim, ed. *Origens do colonialismo português moderno (1822–1891)*. Lisbon: Sá da Costa, 1979.

Amado, Leopoldo. *Guerra colonial e guerra de libertação nacional, 1950–1974: O caso da Guiné-Bissau*. Lisbon: IPAD, 2011.

Andrade, Mário de. *Amílcar Cabral: Essai de biographie politique*. Paris: François Maspero, 1980.

Barata, Victor. "Guiné 63/74–P1668: In memoriam do piloto aviador Baltazar da Silva e de outros portugueses com asas de pássaro (António da Graça Abreu / Luís Graça)." *Luís Graça & camaradas da Guiné* (blog), 17 April 2007. https://blogueforanadaevaotres.blogspot.com/2007/04/guin-6374-p1669-in-memoriam-do-piloto.html.

Bentley, T. Duncan. *Atlantic Islands: Madeira, the Azores, and the Cape Verdes in Seventeenth-Century Commerce and Navigation*. Chicago: University of Chicago Press, 1972.

Boxer, C. R. *Race Relations in the Portuguese Colonial Empire, 1415–1825*. Oxford: Oxford University Press, 1963.

Brito, Eduíno. *A população de Cabo Verde no século XX*. Lisbon: Agência Geral do Ultramar, 1963.

Brito-Semedo, Manuel. "Do nativismo ao nacionalismo: A construção da identidade nacional." In *Cabral no cruzamento de épocas: Comunicações e discursos produzidos no II Simpósio Internacional Amílcar Cabral*, edited by Fundação Amílcar Cabral, 325–39. Praia: Alfa Comunicações, 2005.

Cabral, Amílcar. "Apontamentos sobre poesia caboverdeana." In *Cabo Verde: Boletim de propaganda e informação* (Praia), 3rd year, no. 28 (1 January 1952): 5–8.

————. *Estudos agrários de Amílcar Cabral.* Lisbon/Bissau: Instituto de Investigação Cientifica Tropical/Instituto Nacional de Estudos e Pesquisa, 1988.

————. Foreword to *The Liberation of Guiné: Aspects of an African Revolution*, by Basil Davidson, 9–15. Harmondsworth, UK: Penguin, 1969.

————. Amílcar Cabral, *Return to the Source: Selected Speeches of Amilcar Cabral.* New York: Monthly Review Press, 1973.

————. *Revolution in Guinea: An African People's Struggle.* London: Stage 1, 1970.

————. *Unity and Struggle.* New York: Monthly Review Press, 1979.

————. "The Weapon of Theory." Address to the first Tricontinental Conference of the Peoples of Asia, Africa, and Latin America, Havana, 3 January 1966. https://www.marxists.org/subject/africa/cabral/1966/weapon-theory.htm.

Cabral, Iva, Márcia Souto, and Filinto Elísio, eds. *Cartas de Amílcar Cabral a Maria Helena: A outra face do homem.* Lisbon: Rosa de Porcelana, 2016.

Cabral, Juvenal. *Memórias e reflexões.* 1947, author's edition. Reprint, Praia: Instituto da Biblioteca Nacional, 2002.

Cabral, Luís. *Crónica da libertação.* Lisbon: O Jornal, 1984.

Cabrita Mateus, Dalila. *A PIDE/DGS na guerra colonial (1961–1974).* Lisbon: Terramar, 2004.

Caetano, Marcello. *Depoimento.* Rio de Janeiro: Distribuidora Record, 1974.

————. *Portugal não pode ceder: Discurso pronunciado no Palácio das Necessidades em 6 de Outubro de 1969.* Lisbon: Secretaria de Estado de Informação e Turismo, 1969.

Carreira, António. *Cabo Verde: Formação e extinção de uma sociedade escravocrata (1460–1878).* Bissau: Centro de Estudos da Guiné Portuguesa, 1972.

————. *Migrações nas Ilhas de Cabo Verde.* Lisbon: Universidade Nova de Lisboa, 1977.

Castanheira, José Pedro. *Quem mandou matar Amílcar Cabral?* Lisbon: Relógio d'Água, 1995.

Castro, Fidel. Speech at the Closing Session of the Tricontinental Conference, Havana, 16 January 1966. https://www.marxists.org/history/cuba/archive/castro/1966/01/15.htm.

Chabal, Patrick. *Amílcar Cabral: Revolutionary Leadership and People's War.* New York: Cambridge University Press, 1983.

Chaliand, Gérard. *La pointe du couteau: Mémoires—Tome I.* Paris: Robert Laffont, 2011. Kindle edition.

Chilcote, Ronald H. *Amílcar Cabral's Revolutionary Theory and Practice: A Critical Guide.* Boulder, CO: Lynne Rienner, 1991.

Costa, Eduardo da. "Princípios de administração colonial." In *Antologia colonial portuguesa*, vol. 1, *Política e administração*, 79–96. Lisbon: Agência Geral das Colónias, 1946.

Costa Pereira, A. "Apontamentos sobre a política da Guiné Portuguesa e territórios vizinhos." Report of the Polícia Internacional e de Defesa do Estado (PIDE), 17 January 1963. Available at *Casa comum* (Fundação Mário Soares, Documentos Amílcar Cabral). http://casacomum.org/cc/visualizador?pasta=04999.015.

Crimi, Bruno. "Les assassins de Cabral." *Jeune Afrique*, 3 February 1973, 8–12. Available at *Casa comum* (Fundação Mário Soares, Documentos Amílcar Cabral). http://casacomum.org/cc/visualizador?pasta=07701.005.

Davidson, Basil. *The Fortunate Isles: A Study in African Transformation.* Trenton, NJ: Africa World Press, 1989.

———. *The Liberation of Guiné: Aspects of an African Revolution.* Harmondsworth, UK: Penguin, 1969.

Dhada, Mustafah. *Warriors at Work: How Guinea Was Really Set Free.* Niwot, CO: University Press of Colorado, 1993.

Diggs, Charles. Text quoted in "Tributes to a Fallen Comrade." *Ufahamu: A Journal of African Studies* 3, no. 3 (Winter 1973): 15. http://escholarship.org/uc/item/4vf0v6ws.

Duffy, James. *Portuguese Africa.* Cambridge: Harvard University Press, 1961.

Enes, António. *Moçambique: Relatório apresentado ao governo.* 3rd ed. Lisbon: Agência Geral das Colónias, 1946. First published 1893 by Sociedade de Geographia de Lisboa (Lisbon).

Fanon, Frantz. *The Wretched of the Earth*. Harmondsworth, UK: Penguin, 1967.

Ferreira, J. Pinto, and Miguel Pessoa. "Guiné 63/74–P3859: FAP (6): A Introdução do míssil russo SAM-7 Strela no CTIG." *Luís Graça & camaradas da Guiné* (blog), 9 February 2009. https://blogueforanadaevaotres.blogspot.com/2009/02/guine-6374-p3859-fap-6-introducao-do.html.

Fordham University Modern History Sourcebook. "All-African People's Conference: Resolution on Imperialism and Colonialism, Accra, December 5–13, 1958." https://sourcebooks.fordham.edu/mod/1958-aapc-res1.asp.

Fundação Mário Soares. *Amílcar Cabral: Sou um simples Africano*. Lisbon: Fundação Mário Soares, 2000. Exhibition catalog.

Gleijeses, Piero. "The First Ambassadors: Cuba's Contribution to Guinea-Bissau's War of Independence." *Journal of Latin American Studies* 29, no. 1 (February 1997): 45–88.

Ignatiev, Oleg. *Amílcar Cabral*. Moscow: Edições Progresso, 1984.

———. *Três tiros da PIDE. Quem, porque e como mataram Amílcar Cabral*. Lisbon: Prelo Editora, 1975.

Keesing's. "Repulse of Raids by 'Mercenaries' and Guinean Exiles." *Keesing's Contemporary Archives* 17 (December 1970): 24353. http://web.stanford.edu/group/tomzgroup/pmwiki/uploads/1385-Keesings-1970-12-a-RRW.pdf.

Langley, J. Ayodele. *Pan-Africanism and Nationalism in West Africa, 1900–1945: A Study in Ideology and Social Classes*. Oxford: Clarendon, 1973.

Lara, Lúcio. *Um amplo movimento: Itinerário do MPLA através de documentos e anotações*. Vol. 1. Luanda: Edição Lúcio e Ruth Lara, 1998.

Lopes, Carlos. *Guinea Bissau: From Liberation Struggle to Independent Statehood*. Boulder, CO: Westview Press, 1987.

Lyall, Archibald. *Black and White Make Brown: An Account of a Journey to the Cape Verde Islands and Portuguese Guinea*. London: Heinemann, 1938.

MacQueen, Norrie. "Portugal's First Domino: 'Pluricontinentalism' and Colonial War in Guiné-Bissau, 1963–1974."

Contemporary European History 8, no. 2 (July 1999): 209–30.

Martins, Pedro. *The Testimony of a Freedom Fighter.* 3rd rev. ed. São Vicente, Cape Verde: Gráfica do Mindelo, 2009.

Matos, José. "O Inicio da guerra na Guiné (1961–1964)." *Revista militar,* no. 2566 (November 2015). https://www.revistamilitar.pt/artigo/1066.

Medeiros, Tomás. *A verdadeira morte de Amílcar Cabral.* Lisbon: Althum, 2012.

Mendy, Peter Karibe. *Colonialismo português em África: A tradição da resistência na Guiné-Bissau, 1879–1959.* Lisbon/Bissau: Imprensa Nacional–Casa da Moeda/Instituto Nacional de Estudos e Pesquisa, 1994.

Nkrumah, Kwame. "Speech by the Prime Minister of Ghana at the opening session of the All-African People's Conference, on Monday, December 8, 1958." http://www.columbia.edu/itc/history/mann/w3005/nkrumba.html.

Oramas, Oscar. *Amílcar Cabral: Para além do seu tempo.* Lisbon: Hugin Editores, 1998.

Partido Africano da Independência da Guiné e Cabo Verde. *Sobre o cobarde e criminoso assassinato do nosso querido leader, Amílcar Cabral, fundador e secretario geral do PAIGC: Decisões da direcção do partido.* Conakry: PAIGC, 1973.

Pereira, Aristides. *Uma luta, um partido, dois países: Guiné-Bissau e Cabo Verde.* Lisbon: Editorial Notícias, 2002.

Pereira, Carmen Maria de Araújo. *Os meus três amores.* Bissau: Instituto Nacional de Estudos e Pesquisa, 2016.

Pinto, João Teixeira. *A ocupação militar da Guiné.* Lisbon: Agência Geral das Colónias, 1936.

Ray, Ellen, William Schaap, Karl Van Meter, and Louis Wolf, eds. *Dirty Work 2: The CIA in Africa.* London: Zed Press, 1982.

Robinson, R. A. H. *Contemporary Portugal: A History.* London: George Allen and Unwin, 1979.

Rudebeck, Lars. *Guinea-Bissau: A Study of Political Mobilization.* Uppsala: The Scandinavian Institute of African Studies, 1974.

———. "Reading Cabral on Democracy." In *Africa's Contemporary Challenges: The Legacy of Amilcar Cabral*, edited by Carlos Lopes, 87–96. New York: Routledge, 2010.

Santos, Daniel dos. *Amílcar Cabral: Um outro olhar*. Lisbon: Chiado Editora, 2014.

Silva, João Augusto. *África: Da vida e do amor na selva*. Lisbon: Edições Momento, 1936.

Soares Sousa, Julião. *Amílcar Cabral (1924–1973): Vida e morte de um revolucionàrio africano*. 2nd ed. Lisbon: Nova Vega, 2012.

Sousa Ferreira, Eduardo de. *Portuguese Colonialism in Africa: The End of an Era*. Paris: UNESCO Press, 1974.

Spínola, António de. *Por uma Guiné melhor*. Lisbon: Agência Geral do Ultramar, 1970.

Teixeira da Mota, Avelino. *Guiné Portuguesa*, Volume I: Lisbon: Agência Geral do Ultramar, 1954.

Tomás, António. *O fazedor de utopias: Uma biografia de Amílcar Cabral*. 2nd ed. Lisbon: Edições Tinta-da-China, 2008.

United States Department of State. "Portuguese Guinea: The PAIGC after Amilcar Cabral" (Declassified PA/HO Department of State E.O. 12958). https://2001-2009.state.gov/documents/organization/67534.pdf.

Wauthier, Claude. *The Literature and Thought of Modern Africa: A Survey*. 2nd Eng. lang. ed. London: Heinemann Educational, 1978.